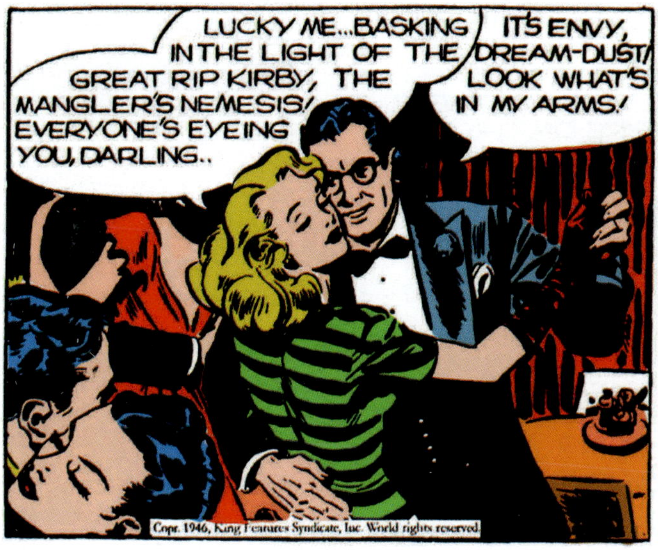
LUCKY ME...BASKING IN THE LIGHT OF THE GREAT RIP KIRBY, THE MANGLER'S NEMESIS! EVERYONE'S EYEING YOU, DARLING..
IT'S ENVY, DREAM-DUST! LOOK WHAT'S IN MY ARMS!
Copr. 1946, King Features Syndicate, Inc. World rights reserved.
I'D FEEL BETTER IF THEY HAD FOUND THE MANGLER'S BODY AND THE HICKS FORMULA I'LL NEVER BE SURE HE'S DEAD.
SILLY! HOW COULD HE HAVE SURVIVED THAT EXPLOSION? HE AND THE FORMULA ARE ON THE RIVER BOTTOM
11-4

OH, RIP... LET'S FORGET THE MANGLER! TONIGHT, LET'S FORGET EVERY-THING BUT US!
EASY, HONEY... SO VERY EASY!
ALEX RAYMOND
RIP! WHAT IS IT?
OH, NOTHING... THAT VOCALIST GAVE ME A START.. SHE REMINDS ME OF PAGAN LEE...

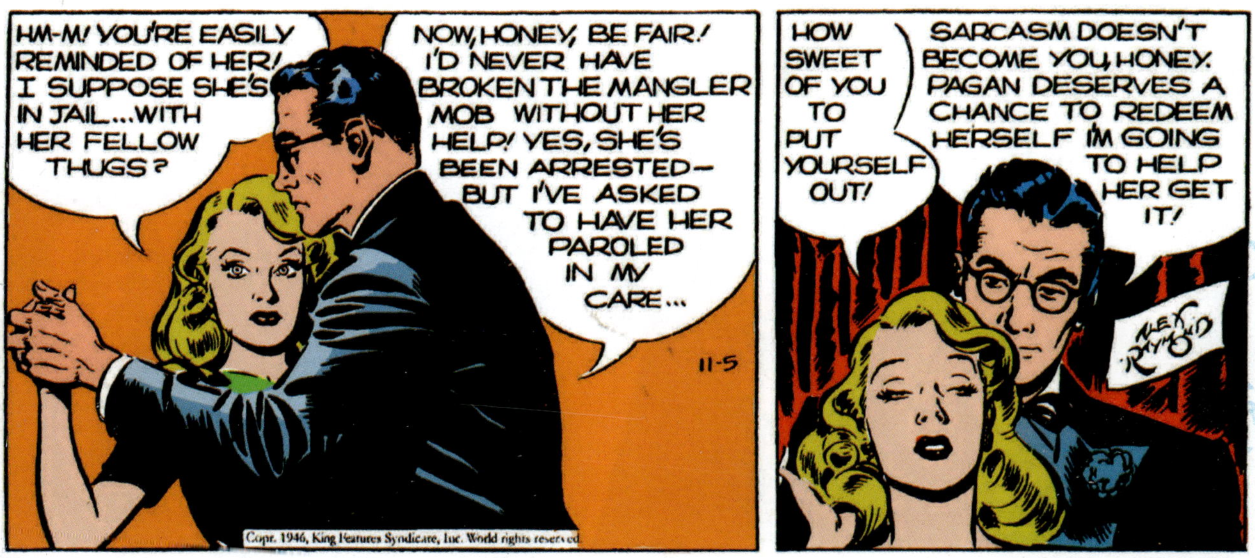
HM-M! YOU'RE EASILY REMINDED OF HER! I SUPPOSE SHE'S IN JAIL...WITH HER FELLOW THUGS?
NOW, HONEY, BE FAIR! I'D NEVER HAVE BROKEN THE MANGLER MOB WITHOUT HER HELP! YES, SHE'S BEEN ARRESTED— BUT I'VE ASKED TO HAVE HER PAROLED IN MY CARE...
11-5
Copr. 1946, King Features Syndicate, Inc. World rights reserved.
HOW SWEET OF YOU TO PUT YOURSELF OUT!
SARCASM DOESN'T BECOME YOU, HONEY. PAGAN DESERVES A CHANCE TO REDEEM HERSELF I'M GOING TO HELP HER GET IT!
ALEX RAYMOND

BETTER STOP EYEIN' THAT BLONDE, SWANEE. KIRBY WON'T LIKE IT!
I'M MORE INTERESTED IN KIRBY. BESIDES, IT'S NONE OF YOUR BUSINESS! GET UP TO THE MIKE... WE'RE ON THE AIR!
11-6
Copr. 1946, King Features Syndicate, Inc. World rights reserved.
OH, RIP! ISN'T SWANEE'S THEME SUPER? THE SINGER IS BONNIE BLUE.
SOUNDS AS IF SHE'S IN PAIN!
PARDON, SIR..BUT SWANEE RIVERS ASKS IF YOU'LL SEE HIM AFTER THE BROADCAST.
SURE... WHY NOT?
ALEX RAYMOND
SWANEE RIVERS IS GOING OFF THE AIR NOW. HE WANTS TO SEE ME IN HIS DRESSING-ROOM AFTERWARDS... COME ON, HONEY..
AH, MR. KIRBY! HOPED YOU'D COME...BUT I WANTED TO SEE YOU ALONE.
THIS IS MISS DORIAN. YOU MAY TALK FREELY..
Copr. 1946, King Features Syndicate, Inc. World rights reserved.

JUST AS YOU SAY, MR. KIRBY. WE WERE GOOD TONIGHT, WEREN'T WE? IN THE GROOVE... MY OWN ARRANGEMENTS, YOU KNOW...
I'M SURE YOU DIDN'T SEND FOR ME TO ASK MY OPINION OF YOUR MUSIC.
11-7
I NEED YOUR HELP, MR. KIRBY. MONEY'S NO OBJECT.
IT IS, TO ME, RIVERS. BUT YOU CAN'T BUY ME. IF I LIKE YOUR CASE, I'LL TAKE IT FOR A FEE...
THE THINGS.. YOU SAY!
MR. KIRBY, I'M BEING BLACKMAILED! SOMEONE IS THREATENING TO DAMAGE MY REPUTATION AND BREAK UP MY HOME, IF I DON'T MEET HIS TERMS, BY DISCLOSING LOVE LETTERS I NEVER WROTE! FORGERIES!
AS ONE OF THE NATION'S TOP BAND LEADERS, I CAN'T AFFORD..
I KNOW YOUR REPUTATION, ALSO YOUR NOTORIETY AS A LADIES' MAN!
THAT'S A LOTTA MALARKEY! THEY MAKE A FUSS OVER ME, YES! BUT I'M NOT SO FOOLISH AS TO WRITE LOVE LETTERS!
WHAT DO YOU WRITE?
CHECKS, MOSTLY.. AND, OF COURSE, AUTO-GRAPHS!
HM-M I'LL HELP YOU, MR. RIVERS. BLACKMAIL'S A NASTY RACKET. COME TO MY OFFICE IN THE MORNING
OH, GOODY!
11-8

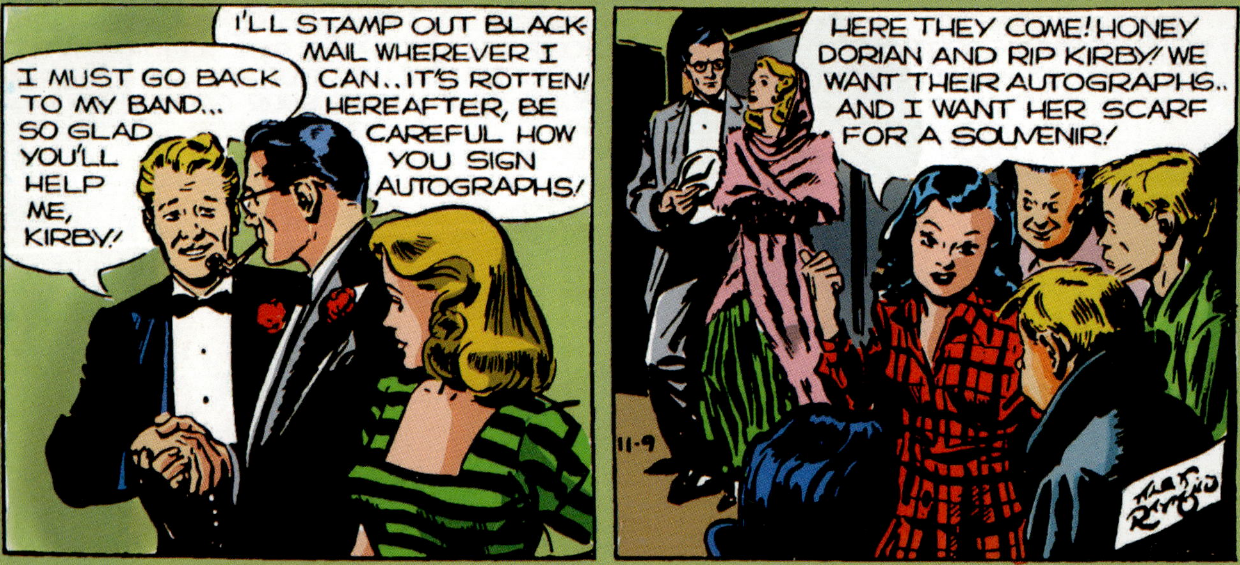
I MUST GO BACK TO MY BAND... SO GLAD YOU'LL HELP ME, KIRBY!
I'LL STAMP OUT BLACK-MAIL WHEREVER I CAN.. IT'S ROTTEN! HEREAFTER, BE CAREFUL HOW YOU SIGN AUTOGRAPHS!
HERE THEY COME! HONEY DORIAN AND RIP KIRBY! WE WANT THEIR AUTOGRAPHS.. AND I WANT HER SCARF FOR A SOUVENIR!
11-9

SORRY, KIDS...NO AUTOGRAPHS...HEY! STOP THAT!
HELP ME, RIP!
GRAB KOIBY'S GLASSES!
Copr. 1946, King Features Syndicate, Inc. World rights reserved.

WHEN RIP DECLINES THE REQUESTS OF A GROUP OF YOUNG AUTOGRAPH SEEKERS, HE AND HONEY ARE SET UPON....
I GOT HER SCARF! LET'S BLOW!
RIP! HELP!
I GOT KIRBY'S... OUCH!
NO, YOU DON'T!

GIVE ME THOSE GLASSES!
YOU LOUSY FLATFOOT!
HEY, YOU STINKERS! COME BACK HERE AND HELP ME!
11-11
ALEX RAYMOND
I FEAR YOUR GENTLEMEN FRIENDS HAVE FLED. CHARMING LITTLE MISS—EH, HONEY?
A BRAT, IF EVER I SAW ONE!

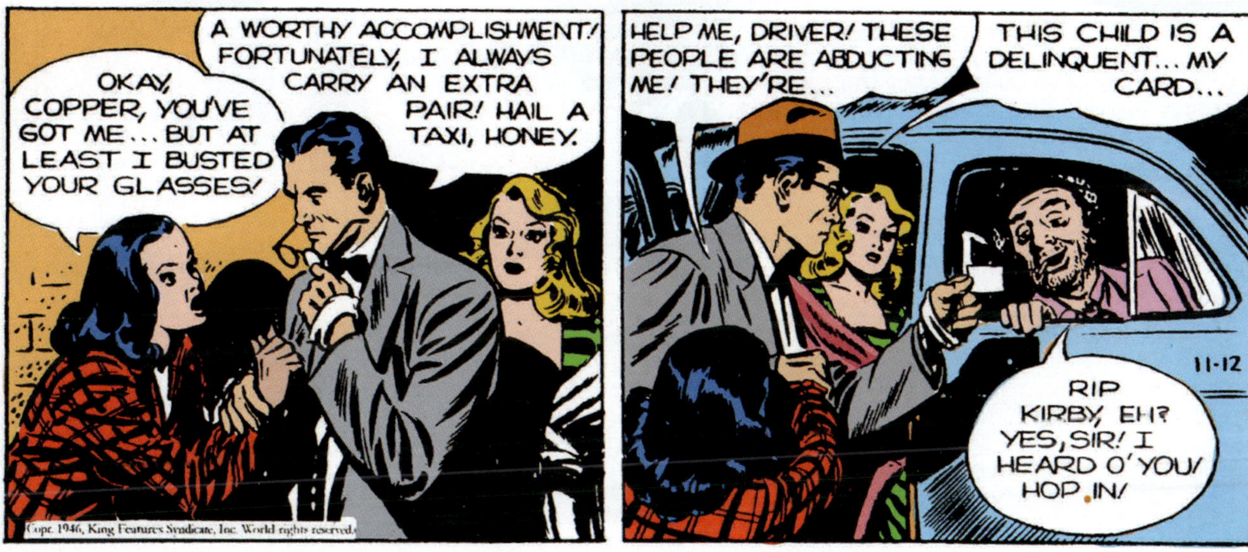
OKAY, COPPER, YOU'VE GOT ME... BUT AT LEAST I BUSTED YOUR GLASSES!
A WORTHY ACCOMPLISHMENT! FORTUNATELY, I ALWAYS CARRY AN EXTRA PAIR! HAIL A TAXI, HONEY.
HELP ME, DRIVER! THESE PEOPLE ARE ABDUCTING ME! THEY'RE...
THIS CHILD IS A DELINQUENT... MY CARD...
11-12
RIP KIRBY, EH? YES, SIR! I HEARD O' YOU! HOP IN!

YOU SEE THE POWER OF A GOOD REPUTATION?
STOP PREACHIN'! A GUN WOULDA GOT THE SAME RESULTS! YOU SMUG, SOLID CITIZENS GIMME A PAIN!
HONESTLY, RIP, I'M GOING TO FORGET I'M A LADY AND BELT HER ONE!
ALEX RAYMOND
LET'S STOP FOR COFFEE BEFORE GOING TO HEADQUARTERS.
HEADQUARTERS! THAT'S A JOKE! HOW LONG D'YA THINK THEY'LL HOLD ME FOR BUSTIN' YOUR GLASSES? YOU GOT NOTHIN' ON ME!
ANGEL CHILD SEEMS WISE BEYOND HER YEARS, RIP!

HUNGRY, WEREN'T YOU?
WHAT'S SO STRANGE ABOUT THAT? TASTES ALL THE BETTER 'CAUSE YOU'RE PAYIN' FOR IT! SUCKER!
HONESTLY, RIP.. WHAT KIND OF HOMES DO BRATS LIKE THESE COME FROM, ANYWAY?
Copr. 1946, King Features Syndicate, Inc. World rights reserved.
OH, BROTHER! HERE IT COMES! GO AHEAD.. TAKE ME APART! SEE WHAT MAKES ME CLICK!
DON'T TEMPT US, DARLING!
ALEX RAYMOND 11-13
WHY DON'T YOU WISE UP? YOU HAVE YOUTH, LOOKS, AND APPEAR INTELLIGENT... EVERYTHING NECESSARY FOR SUCCESS AND HAPPINESS. BELIEVE ME, THE PATH YOU'RE FOLLOWING LEADS ONLY TO GRIEF...
Copr. 1946, King Features Syndicate, Inc. World rights reserved.
I'M NOT GOING TO ARREST YOU. YOU'RE FREE TO FOLLOW THE PATH YOU WISH. GOOD NIGHT.. AND GOOD LUCK!
RIP, YOU'VE GOT A LOT TO LEARN ABOUT WOMEN! THAT GIRL'S BAD, CLEAN THROUGH! FIRST, PAGAN LEE—NOW, THIS ONE! RIP KIRBY, GOOD SAMARITAN TO BAD WOMEN!
TOUCHÈ, HONEY. LET'S GO.. I'M TIRED.
11-14
ALEX RAYMOND
WE THOUGHT YOU WUZ DONE FOR!
WHEN WE SEEN KOIBY GRAB YA, I GOT AWAY... AN' SMALL THANKS TO YOU COWARDS! DID YOU GET HONEY DORIAN'S SCARF?
YEAH

SNAZZY, HUH?
HUBBA, HUBBA! WHAT'S UNDER IT AIN'T BAD, EITHER! GONNA GIMME A KISS FER GETTIN' IT FOR YA?
ALEX RAYMOND
Copr. 1946, King Features Syndicate, Inc. World rights
PICK UP THE SLOB AND LET'S BE SHOVIN'! THE OLD MAN'LL HAVE FITS IF I AIN'T IN BEFORE DAWN!
YA MEAN TO SAY THESE ARE THE ONLY AUTOGRAPHS YA GOT ALL EVENING? THIRD-RATE CELEBRITIES! HAS-BEENS! NOT A DOLLAR SIGN IN THE LOT!
WE COVERED THE USUAL PLACES, SPIDER. THE CORK .. GLITTER CLUB, AN' THE REST. ALMOST GOT RIP KIRBY AN' HONEY DORIAN.
KIRBY, EH? HIS AUTOGRAPH MIGHT PROVE USEFUL! WOULDN'T HE GIVE?
WE MIGHT'VE COAXED HIM.. BUT HE GOT MAD WHEN PORKY SWIPED HIS GIRL FRIEND'S SCARF..
Copr. 1946, King Features Syndicate, Inc. World rights reserved.
AN' YOU'RE WEARIN' IT, AIN'TCHA, SILKY? YOU PUT PORKY UP TO IT! NO WONDER KIRBY GOT SORE! I OUGHTTA KILL YOU! GET OUTTA HERE AN' GET ME SOME NAMES! AN' KIRBY'S BETTER BE AMONG 'EM!
11-16
ALEX RAYMOND

IF WE DON'T GET SPECIMENS OF IMPORTANT PEOPLE'S HANDWRITING, WE DON'T EAT. AND IN AS PRECARIOUS A PROFESSION AS OURS, IT NEVER HURTS TO HAVE THE SIGNATURE OF A BIG EYE LIKE KIRBY ON FILE!
IF YOU AND THOSE GUTTER-SNIPE PALS OF YOURS DON'T STOP ROUGHING UP CELEBRITIES, YOU'LL RUIN OUR PITCH! WE WANT AUTOGRAPHS, NOT SAMPLES OF THEIR WEARING APPAREL! TAKE HONEY DORIAN'S SCARF BACK TO KIRBY, APOLOGIZE, AND GET HIS SIGNATURE!
ALEX RAYMOND
11-18

FROM NOW ON YOU'D BETTER DO JUST AS OLD SPIDER GRUNT SAYS! UNDERSTAND, LITTLE ONE?
Y'YES, SPIDER, I WILL... I WILL!
Copr. 1946, King Features Syndicate, Inc. World rights reserved.
A MISS...AH.. SILKY SHAW TO SEE YOU, SIR...
SILKY, EH? WHERE DO THEY GET THESE CORNY NICKNAMES? OKAY... SHOW HER IN, DESMOND.

OH... IT'S YOU!
YES, MR. KIRBY, I... I CAME TO APOLOGIZE FOR BEING SUCH A BRAT LAST NIGHT. I BROUGHT BACK MISS DORIAN'S SCARF... THE ONE PORKY SWIPED...
THANKS. AREN'T YOU UNDERGOING A RATHER SUDDEN CHANGE OF HEART, KIDDO?
I...I'VE BEEN DOING A LOT OF THINKING, MR. KIRBY.. I'VE DECIDED I'D LIKE TO BE THE KIND OF GIRL YOU ADMIRE..
Copr. 1946, King Features Syndicate, Inc. World rights reserved.
BEFORE I GO, MR. KIRBY, COULD I PLEASE HAVE YOUR AUTOGRAPH.. I'LL TREASURE IT...
WELL... IF IT MEANS SO MUCH TO YOU...
ALEX RAYMOND
11-19

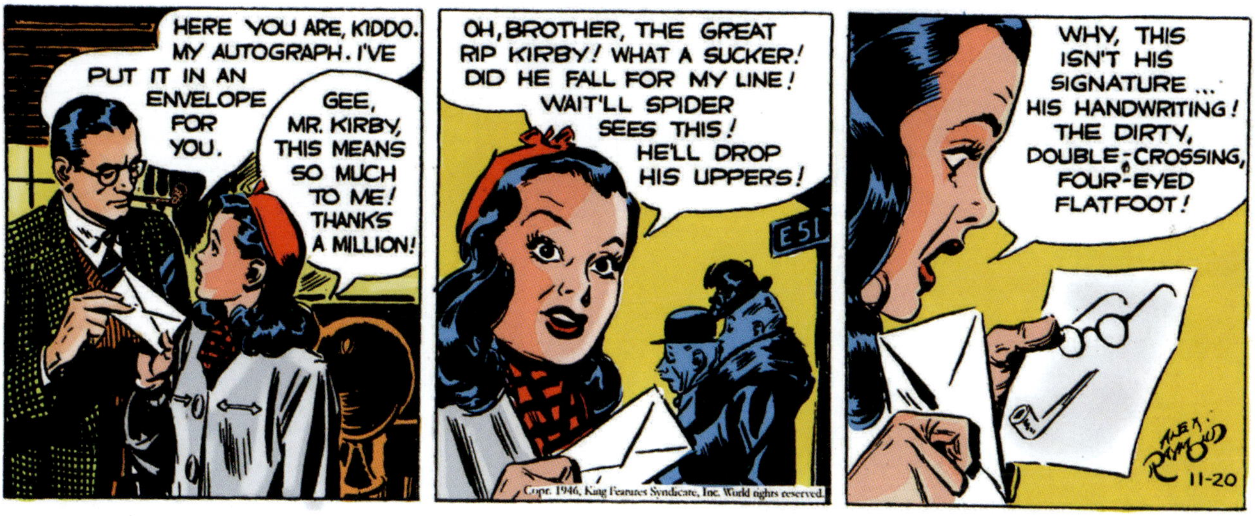
HERE YOU ARE, KIDDO. MY AUTOGRAPH. I'VE PUT IT IN AN ENVELOPE FOR YOU.
GEE, MR. KIRBY, THIS MEANS SO MUCH TO ME! THANKS A MILLION!
OH, BROTHER, THE GREAT RIP KIRBY! WHAT A SUCKER! DID HE FALL FOR MY LINE! WAIT'LL SPIDER SEES THIS! HE'LL DROP HIS UPPERS!
E 51
Copr. 1946, King Features Syndicate, Inc. World rights reserved.
WHY, THIS ISN'T HIS SIGNATURE... HIS HANDWRITING! THE DIRTY, DOUBLE-CROSSING, FOUR-EYED FLATFOOT!
ALEX RAYMOND
11-20

HM-M! MISS SILKY SHAW SEEMS A BIT PERTURBED. HONEY'S RIGHT.. I DON'T KNOW MUCH ABOUT WOMEN, BUT I KNOW A VIXEN WHEN I SEE ONE!
SO YA LET KIRBY PALM THIS OFF ON YA AS HIS AUTOGRAPH! I WANTED HIS SIGNATURE, STUPID!
WELL.. IT IS AN AUTOGRAPH.. BUT THE RAT CROSSED ME UP!

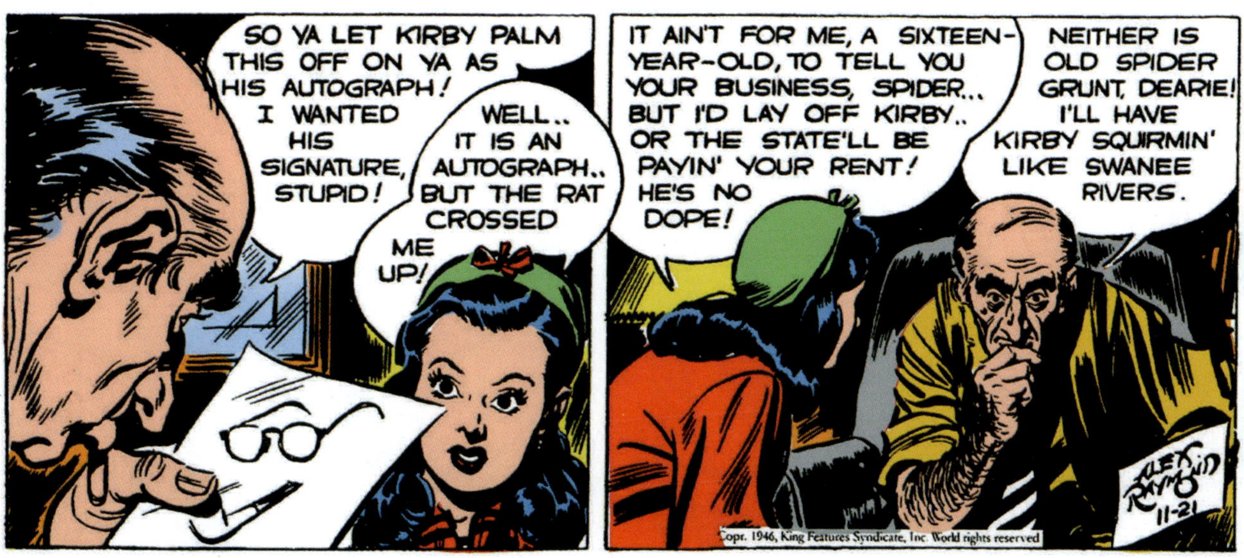
SO YA LET KIRBY PALM THIS OFF ON YA AS HIS AUTOGRAPH! I WANTED HIS SIGNATURE, STUPID!
WELL.. IT IS AN AUTOGRAPH.. BUT THE RAT CROSSED ME UP!
IT AIN'T FOR ME, A SIXTEEN-YEAR-OLD, TO TELL YOU YOUR BUSINESS, SPIDER... BUT I'D LAY OFF KIRBY.. OR THE STATE'LL BE PAYIN' YOUR RENT! HE'S NO DOPE!
NEITHER IS OLD SPIDER GRUNT, DEARIE! I'LL HAVE KIRBY SQUIRMIN' LIKE SWANEE RIVERS.
ALEX RAYMOND
11-21
Copr. 1946, King Features Syndicate, Inc. World rights reserved

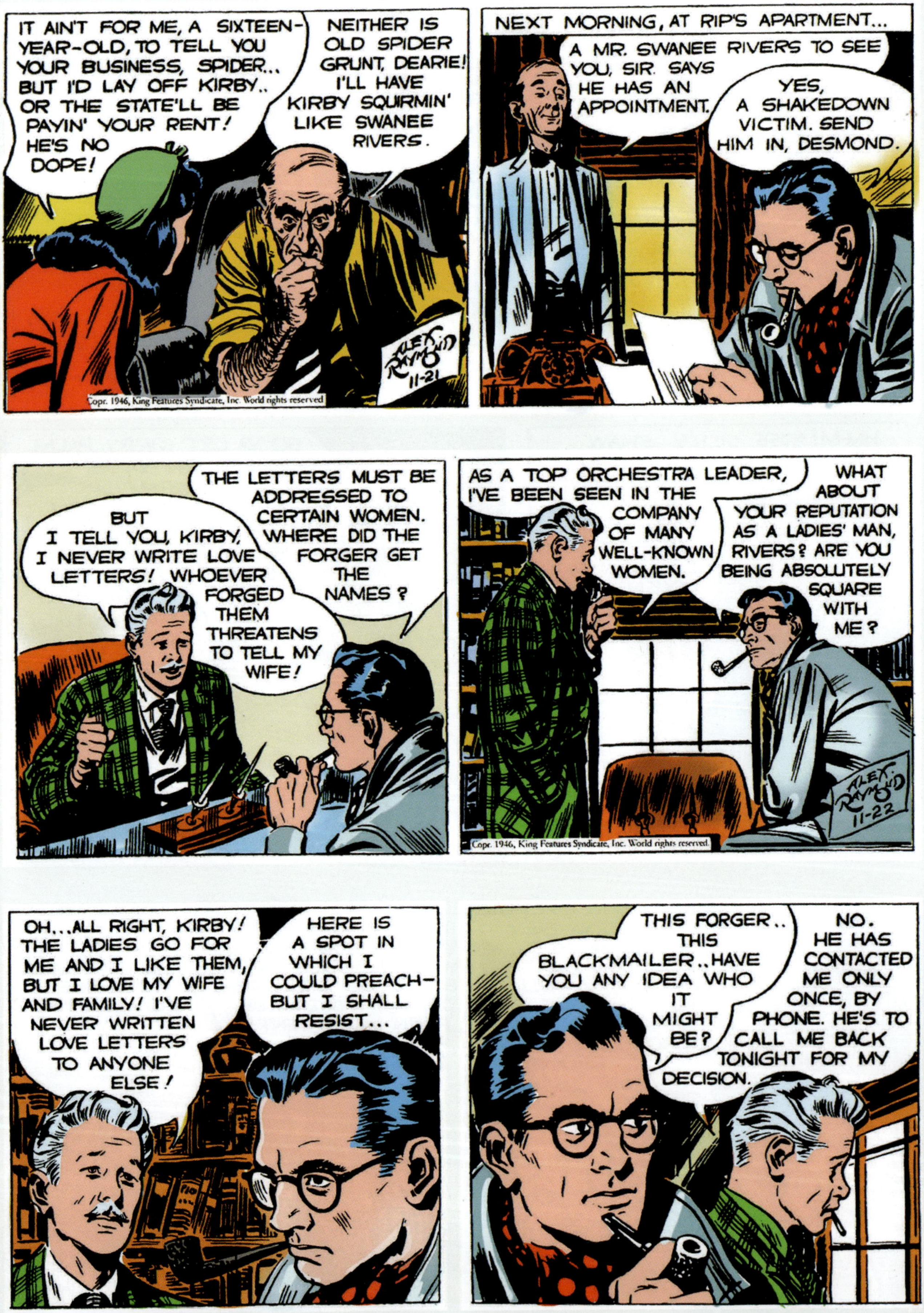
IT AIN'T FOR ME, A SIXTEEN-YEAR-OLD, TO TELL YOU YOUR BUSINESS, SPIDER... BUT I'D LAY OFF KIRBY.. OR THE STATE'LL BE PAYIN' YOUR RENT! HE'S NO DOPE!
NEITHER IS OLD SPIDER GRUNT, DEARIE! I'LL HAVE KIRBY SQUIRMIN' LIKE SWANEE RIVERS.
ALEX RAYMOND 11-21
Copr. 1946, King Features Syndicate, Inc. World rights reserved
NEXT MORNING, AT RIP'S APARTMENT...
A MR. SWANEE RIVERS TO SEE YOU, SIR. SAYS HE HAS AN APPOINTMENT.
YES, A SHAKEDOWN VICTIM. SEND HIM IN, DESMOND.
BUT I TELL YOU, KIRBY, I NEVER WRITE LOVE LETTERS! WHOEVER FORGED THEM THREATENS TO TELL MY WIFE!
THE LETTERS MUST BE ADDRESSED TO CERTAIN WOMEN. WHERE DID THE FORGER GET THE NAMES?
AS A TOP ORCHESTRA LEADER, I'VE BEEN SEEN IN THE COMPANY OF MANY WELL-KNOWN WOMEN.
WHAT ABOUT YOUR REPUTATION AS A LADIES' MAN, RIVERS? ARE YOU BEING ABSOLUTELY SQUARE WITH ME?
ALEX RAYMOND 11-22
Copr. 1946, King Features Syndicate, Inc. World rights reserved.
OH...ALL RIGHT, KIRBY! THE LADIES GO FOR ME AND I LIKE THEM, BUT I LOVE MY WIFE AND FAMILY! I'VE NEVER WRITTEN LOVE LETTERS TO ANYONE ELSE!
HERE IS A SPOT IN WHICH I COULD PREACH- BUT I SHALL RESIST...
THIS FORGER.. THIS BLACKMAILER..HAVE YOU ANY IDEA WHO IT MIGHT BE?
NO. HE HAS CONTACTED ME ONLY ONCE, BY PHONE. HE'S TO CALL ME BACK TONIGHT FOR MY DECISION.

IF, AS YOU SAY, YOU'VE NEVER WRITTEN ANY LOVE LETTERS, HOW DO YOU KNOW THIS WHOLE THING ISN'T A HOAX?
HE SENT ME THIS PHOTOSTAT OF THE LOWER PORTION OF A LETTER, SHOWING MY SIGNATURE.
Copr. 1946, King Features Syndicate, Inc. World rights reserved.
IT'S A CLEVER FORGERY. MUCH AS MY WIFE LOVES ME, SHE'D NEVER BELIEVE I DIDN'T WRITE IT. I CAN'T TAKE THAT CHANCE, KIRBY.
THEN, FOR THE TIME BEING, RIVERS, YOU'LL HAVE TO PLAY ALONG WITH THIS BLACKMAILER. KEEP ME ADVISED.. WE MAY BE ABLE TO SET A TRAP...
ALEX RAYMOND 11-23

I KNOW YOU DON'T THINK MUCH OF ME, KIRBY... BUT IT ISN'T ME I'M ASKING YOU TO DEFEND. LET'S RUN OUT TO MY HOME..
ENTIRELY UNNECESSARY. I'VE ALREADY AGREED TO HELP YOU...BUT A DRIVE IN THE COUNTRY WOULD BE NICE...
Copr. 1946, King Features Syndicate, Inc. World rights reserved.
IF YOU DIDN'T WRITE THOSE LOVE LETTERS RIVERS, WHY NOT EXPLAIN THE WHOLE BUSINESS TO YOUR WIFE? THAT WOULD PULL THE BLACKMAILER'S TEETH AND YOU WOULDN'T NEED ME.
I CAN'T RISK HER DISBELIEF, KIRBY. SHE LOVES ME BUT SHE ALSO KNOWS ME... AND MY WEAKNESSES.

RATIONAL ENOUGH..BUT I DON'T THINK WE QUITE REALIZE HOW IRRATIONAL LOVE CAN BE. LET'S GO.
YOUR AUTOGRAPH, MR. KIRBY?
SORRY, SON..
MY CAR'S OVER THIS WAY..
ALEX RAYMOND 11-25
TRIED TO GET KIRBY'S AUTOGRAPH LIKE YOU SAID, SPIDER. NO SOAP. HE WAS IN A HURRY. GOIN' SOMEWHERE WITH SWANEE RIVERS..
SO RIVERS IS WHININ' TO KIRBY, IS HE?

I'M SCARED, SPIDER! IF SWANEE RIVERS HAS HIRED KIRBY, WE'D BETTER LAY OFF!
WE NEED THE MOOLA, SILKY.. AN' I AIN'T DROPPIN' A SURE THING! I TOLD THE LOUSE TO STAY AWAY FROM THE COPS! HE'LL SQUIRM FER THIS!
IN THE CONNECTICUT HILLS...
HERE WE ARE, KIRBY... MY HOME!
MODEST LITTLE HEAP, RIVERS.
ALEX RAYMOND 11-26
Copr. 1946, King Features Syndicate, Inc. World rights reserved.

IN SOME WAYS, KIRBY, I'M A WEAK NO-GOOD. BUT THIS PART OF MY LIFE I'D DIE TO DEFEND! NO SHAME, NO SCANDAL MUST TOUCH IT!
Copr. 1946, King Features Syndicate, Inc. World rights reserved.
SWANEE! DARLING!
POP! GIMME A KISS, POP!
I'M NEXT, YA JERK! LADIES FIRST!

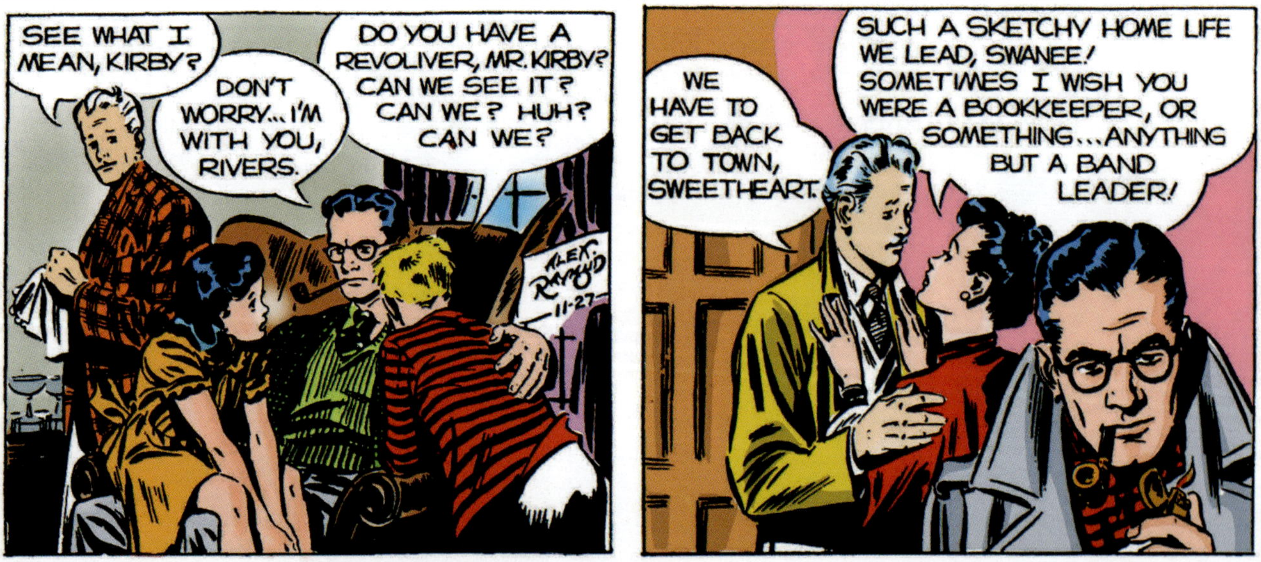
SEE WHAT I MEAN, KIRBY?
DON'T WORRY... I'M WITH YOU, RIVERS.
DO YOU HAVE A REVOLIVER, MR. KIRBY? CAN WE SEE IT? CAN WE? HUH? CAN WE?
ALEX RAYMOND 11-27
WE HAVE TO GET BACK TO TOWN, SWEETHEART.
SUCH A SKETCHY HOME LIFE WE LEAD, SWANEE! SOMETIMES I WISH YOU WERE A BOOKKEEPER, OR SOMETHING... ANYTHING BUT A BAND LEADER!

G'BYE, POP. COME SOON AGAIN.. AN' BRING MR. KIRBY, WILLYA?
YEAH! HUBBA, HUBBA!
ALEX RAYMOND
11-28
Copr. 1946, King Features Syndicate, Inc. World rights reserved.
RIVERS, YOU'RE A LUCKY MAN TO HAVE SUCH A FAMILY. TO PROTECT THEM, YOU'D BETTER PLAY ALONG WITH THIS BLACKMAILER. I'LL HELP ALL I CAN.
LUCKY— AND A FOOL! ONLY A FOOL WOULD BE IN SUCH A FIX!
SO YA WENT AN' SPILLED TO KIRBY, DID YA, RIVERS? GOIN' TO THE COPS WILL COST YA DOUBLE!
NO! I DIDN'T! KIRBY IS A FRIEND OF MINE!
Copr. 1946, King Features Syndicate, Inc. World rights reserved.
Y'RE A LIAR! YER STUPIDITY WILL COST YA TWENTY THOUSAND DOLLARS! CARRY THE CASH ON YER PERSON! ONE O' MY AGENTS WILL CONTACT YA!
BUT I.. HELLO! HELLO! HE HUNG UP!
BUT, KIRBY! TWENTY THOUSAND! IT'S TOO MUCH!
YOU'D BETTER DO IT, RIVERS. YOU'VE GOT TO GET THOSE FORGED LETTERS. I'LL HAVE YOU TAILED...
ALEX RAYMOND
11-29
I KNOW IT'S EARLY, DESMOND, BUT YOU AND I WILL HAVE TO ALTERNATE TAILING SWANEE RIVERS. YOU KNOW WHAT TO DO IF YOU SEE RIVERS SWAPPING PACKAGES WITH ANYONE. GET GOING.
ON MY WAY, MR. KIRBY.
Copr. 1946, King Features Syndicate, Inc. World rights reserved.

OUTSIDE SWANEE RIVERS'S APARTMENT...
WHO IS IT?
TELEGRAM, FOR MR. RIVERS.
WESTERN UNION
UGH! YOU'RE AN EARLY BIRD, SON! YOU AWAKENED ME...WHAT'S COOKIN'?
I GOT A PACKAGE FOR YOU. IT'LL COST YA TWENTY GRAND! I AIN'T FROM WESTERN UNION..IF YA KNOW WHAT I MEAN...
ALEX RAYMOND 11-30
ONE OF SPIDER GRUNT'S JUVENILE AGENTS HAS CALLED UPON SWANEE RIVERS FOR THE BLACKMAIL MONEY.
I AIN'T FROM WESTERN UNION AN' I AIN'T TELLIN' WHO SENT ME! YA GET THIS PACKAGE WHEN I GET THE TWENTY GRAND!
YOU CORRUPT LITTLE PUNK!
I'LL BE DARNED IF I'LL GIVE HIM TWENTY GRAND FOR A BUNCH OF FORGED LOVE LETTERS..KIRBY'S ADVICE TO THE CONTRARY! I'LL PAY TEN THOUSAND...THE ORIGINAL FIGURE..
IT'S IN SMALL BILLS AND RATHER BULKY, SO I WRAPPED IT UP...
IT BETTER BE ALL HERE, BUD! MY BOSS IS ROUGH ON CHARACTERS WHO TRY TO SLIP ONE OVER ON HIM!
Copr. 1946, King Features Syndicate, Inc. World rights reserved.
MEANWHILE DESMOND ENTERS RIVERS'S APARTMENT BUILDING, UNDER RIP'S INSTRUCTIONS TO GUARD THE BAND LEADER.
ALEX RAYMOND 12-2

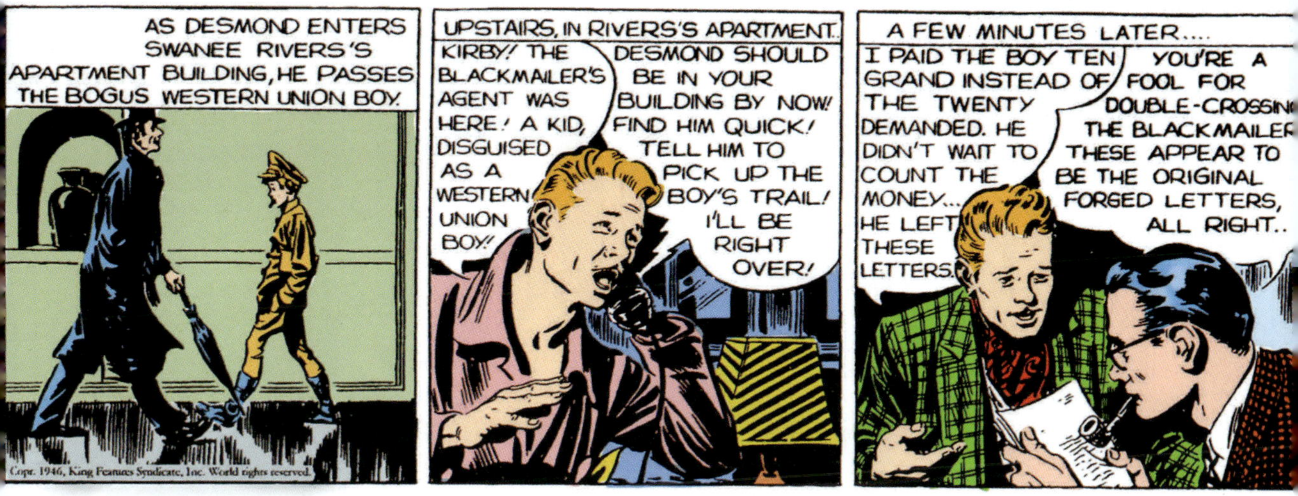
AS DESMOND ENTERS SWANEE RIVERS'S APARTMENT BUILDING, HE PASSES THE BOGUS WESTERN UNION BOY.
Copr. 1946, King Features Syndicate, Inc. World rights reserved.
UPSTAIRS, IN RIVERS'S APARTMENT.
KIRBY! THE BLACKMAILER'S AGENT WAS HERE! A KID, DISGUISED AS A WESTERN UNION BOY!
DESMOND SHOULD BE IN YOUR BUILDING BY NOW! FIND HIM QUICK! TELL HIM TO PICK UP THE BOY'S TRAIL! I'LL BE RIGHT OVER!
A FEW MINUTES LATER....
I PAID THE BOY TEN GRAND INSTEAD OF THE TWENTY DEMANDED. HE DIDN'T WAIT TO COUNT THE MONEY... HE LEFT THESE LETTERS.
YOU'RE A FOOL FOR DOUBLE-CROSSING THE BLACKMAILER. THESE APPEAR TO BE THE ORIGINAL FORGED LETTERS, ALL RIGHT..

MEANWHILE, DESMOND, IN A TAXI, SCOURS THE STREETS AROUND RIVERS'S APARTMENT, LOOKING FOR THE BOGUS WESTERN UNION BOY.
ALEX RAYMOND 12-3
I COMBED THE STREETS, SIR...NOT A WESTERN UNION BOY IN SIGHT!
GOT AWAY, EH? TOO BAD, DESMOND. OUR ONLY HOPE NOW IS THAT THE BLACKMAILER WILL TRY TO CONTACT YOU AGAIN, RIVERS, FOR THE TEN THOUSAND YOU HELD OUT ON HIM..
Copr. 1946, King Features Syndicate, Inc., World rights reserved.

YOU DOUBLE-CROSSED ME, RIVERS! YOU ONLY SENT ME TEN THOUSAND BUCKS! IF YOU'RE SMART YOU'LL CARRY THAT OTHER TEN ON YOUR PERSON...
ALEX RAYMOND 12-4
THE FAKE WESTERN UNION BOY HAS DELIVERED THE BLACKMAIL MONEY TO HIS BOSS, SPIDER GRUNT.
..I'M GONNA CONTACT YOU AGAIN! AN' I'M WARNIN' YOU, KIRBY BETTER NOT BE WITH YOU..OR YOU'LL TAKE THE CONSEQUENCES! I'LL BE SEEIN' YOU!
WAIT! HELLO! HELLO! HE HUNG UP!

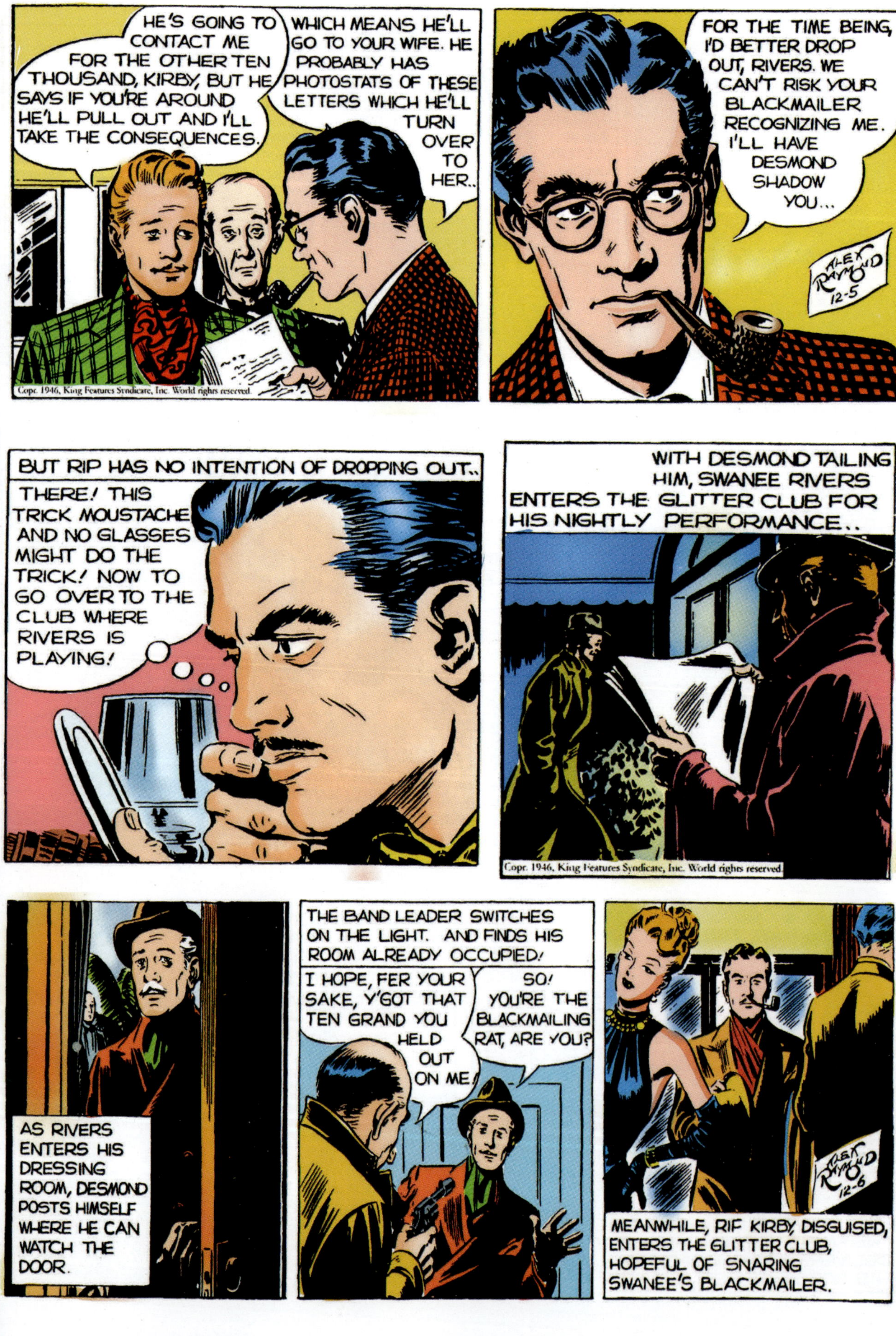
HE'S GOING TO CONTACT ME FOR THE OTHER TEN THOUSAND, KIRBY, BUT HE SAYS IF YOU'RE AROUND HE'LL PULL OUT AND I'LL TAKE THE CONSEQUENCES.
WHICH MEANS HE'LL GO TO YOUR WIFE. HE PROBABLY HAS PHOTOSTATS OF THESE LETTERS WHICH HE'LL TURN OVER TO HER..
Copr. 1946, King Features Syndicate, Inc. World rights reserved.
FOR THE TIME BEING, I'D BETTER DROP OUT, RIVERS. WE CAN'T RISK YOUR BLACKMAILER RECOGNIZING ME. I'LL HAVE DESMOND SHADOW YOU...
ALEX RAYMOND 12-5
BUT RIP HAS NO INTENTION OF DROPPING OUT..
THERE! THIS TRICK MOUSTACHE AND NO GLASSES MIGHT DO THE TRICK! NOW TO GO OVER TO THE CLUB WHERE RIVERS IS PLAYING!
WITH DESMOND TAILING HIM, SWANEE RIVERS ENTERS THE GLITTER CLUB FOR HIS NIGHTLY PERFORMANCE..
Copr. 1946, King Features Syndicate, Inc. World rights reserved.
AS RIVERS ENTERS HIS DRESSING ROOM, DESMOND POSTS HIMSELF WHERE HE CAN WATCH THE DOOR.
THE BAND LEADER SWITCHES ON THE LIGHT. AND FINDS HIS ROOM ALREADY OCCUPIED!
I HOPE, FER YOUR SAKE, Y'GOT THAT TEN GRAND YOU HELD OUT ON ME.
SO! YOU'RE THE BLACKMAILING RAT, ARE YOU?
ALEX RAYMOND 12-6
MEANWHILE, RIP KIRBY, DISGUISED, ENTERS THE GLITTER CLUB, HOPEFUL OF SNARING SWANEE'S BLACKMAILER.

SO YOU'RE THE FORGER! THE RAT WHO'S BEEN BLACKMAILING ME.
SHUT UP AN' HAND OVER THAT TEN GRAND!
YOU'RE THE MISERABLE LOW-LIFE WHO THREATENS THE HAPPINESS OF MY WIFE AND CHILDREN.
NOT IF YA COME THROUGH WITH THAT OTHER TEN THOUSAND! CUT THE DRAMATICS.. I AIN'T GOT MUCH TIME!
Copr. 1946, King Features Syndicate, Inc., World rights reserved.
RIVERS'S HAND GOES TO HIS POCKET, BUT EMERGES WITH A GUN! SPIDER GRUNT FIRES THROUGH HIS POCKET...
IDIOT! GOOD THING MY ROD HAS A SILENCER! IT'S ALL HERE! TEN THOUSAND! NOW TO GET OUTTA HERE!
ALEX RAYMOND 12-7
AT THE FAMOUS GLITTER CLUB THE STAGE IS SET FOR THE SWANEE RIVERS BROADCAST.
WHAT IN BLAZES IS KEEPING RIVERS? WE'RE ON THE AIR IN TEN MINUTES.
I'LL SEE IF HE'S IN HIS DRESSING ROOM.
AT HIS TABLE THE DISGUISED RIP KIRBY GROWS APPREHENSIVE...
ALMOST BROADCAST TIME! I DON'T LIKE THIS!
DESMOND FIDGETS NERVOUSLY AT HIS POST OUTSIDE RIVERS'S DRESSING ROOM.
WHY DOESN'T HE COME OUT? ALMOST TIME FOR HIS RADIO SHOW!
ALEX RAYMOND 12-9
BUT SWANEE RIVERS WILL NEVER BROADCAST AGAIN...
THE FOOL WENT FOR HIS GUN! WELL, I'VE GOT THE TEN GRAND... NOW TO GET OUTTA HERE!
Copr. 1946, King Features Syndicate, Inc. World rights reserved.

OUTSIDE SWANEE RIVERS'S DRESSING ROOM AT THE GLITTER CLUB.
SWANEE! IT'S ME, BONNIE..YOUR VOCALIST! WE'RE ON THE AIR IN A FEW MINUTES!
NO ANSWER! BUT I SAW HIM GO IN...
SWANEE! SWANEE! OPEN UP!
MR. KIRBY! I HARDLY KNEW YOU IN THAT DISGUISE! I TAILED RIVERS HERE..HE WENT INTO HIS DRESSING ROOM.
BACK...I'LL SMASH THE DOOR IN!
A FIGURE EMERGES FROM SWANEE'S DRESSING-ROOM WINDOW INTO AN ALLEY...
GEE, SPIDER! IT TOOK YOU LONG ENOUGH! DID YOU GET THE DOUGH?
HERE, SILKY.. GRAB IT AN' RUN! I HADDA KNOCK HIM OFF! SEE YA AT THE HIDE-OUT!
ALEX RAYMOND 12-10
Copr. 1946, King Features Syndicate, Inc. World rights reserved.
THE DISGUISED RIP KIRBY SMASHES INTO SWANEE RIVERS'S DRESSING ROOM...
DEAD! MURDERED! HIS WALLET IS MISSING!
THIS WINDOW OVERLOOKING THE ALLEY IS OPEN, MR. KIRBY..
ALEX RAYMOND 12-11
Copr 1946, King Features Syndicate, Inc., World rights reserved
AS I SEE IT, THE BLACKMAILER, WHOEVER HE'S, ENTERED THROUGH THE WINDOW. RIVERS DREW HIS GUN AND WAS SHOT. THE MURDERER'S GUN MUST HAVE HAD A SILENCER, OR WE'D HAVE HEARD IT. SEARCH THE ALLEY, DESMOND...I'LL CALL THE POLICE!

SPIDER GRUNT'S HIDE-OUT...
WHY'D YOU KILL RIVERS, SPIDER? THE EXTRA TEN GRAND WASN'T WORTH IT! BLACKMAIL'S ONE THING..BUT MURDER....!
USE YER HEAD, SILKY! I HADDA DO IT! HE PULLED A GUN ON ME! WE BETTER GET OUTTA TOWN TILL THIS THING BLOWS OVER!
I CERTAINLY FUMBLED THE BALL, DESMOND! RIVERS COUNTED ON ME AND LOST HIS LIFE! I DON'T KNOW WHO THE BLACKMAIL-MURDERER IS.. DON'T EVEN HAVE A CLUE!
ALEX RAYMOND 12-12
DON'T BE TOO HARD ON YOURSELF, SIR. YOU CERTAINLY TOOK EVERY PRECAUTION
I SHOULD DRIVE OUT AND SEE RIVERS'S WIFE. I'LL CALL HONEY DORIAN AND ASK HER TO GO WITH ME.
Copr. 1946, King Features Syndicate, Inc., World rights reserved
AT THE MURDERED SWANEE RIVERS'S COUNTRY HOME.
I'M DREADFULLY SORRY, MRS. RIVERS. I'LL GET THE MURDERER IF IT TAKES THE REST OF MY DAYS! WHAT MORE CAN I SAY?
MY DEAR SWANEE! I LOVED HIM SO! HE WAS SO SWEET... SO KIND...
HOW AWFUL, RIP! MRS. RIVERS IS SO LOVELY... AND THOSE SWEET CHILDREN...
I LET THEM DOWN, HONEY. I FAILED TO PROTECT RIVERS ADEQUATELY! BUT I'LL AVENGE HIM! SO HELP ME, I WILL!
ALEX RAYMOND 12-13
Copr. 1946, King Features Syndicate, Inc., World rights reserved
WHY, RIP, DARLING! YOU'RE CRYING!
ME? DON'T BE SILLY! JUST... SMOKE IN MY EYES!

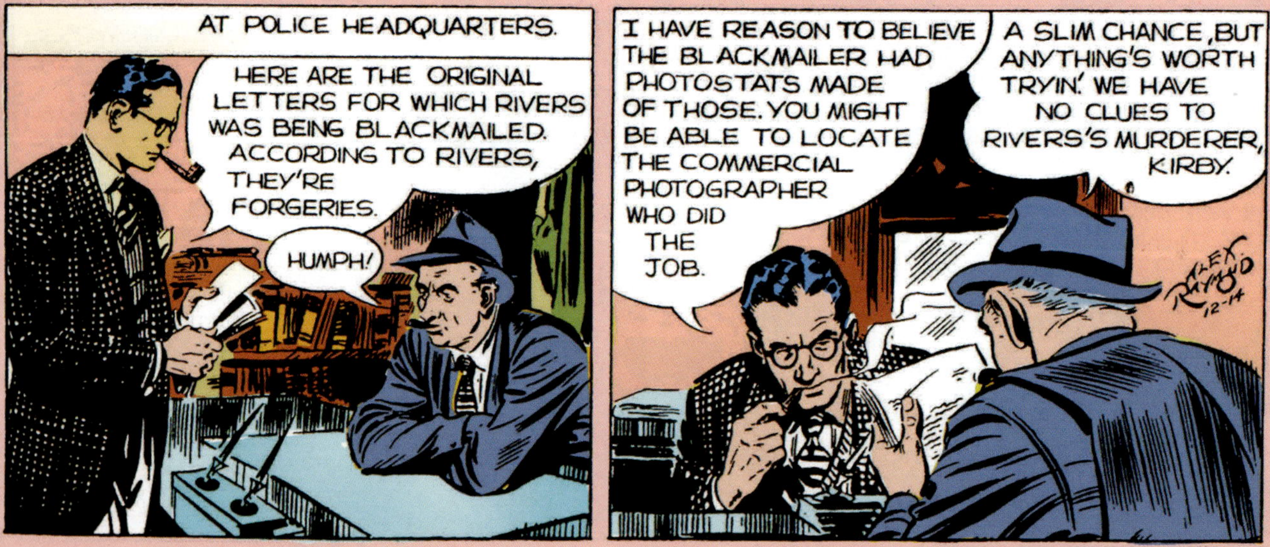
AT POLICE HEADQUARTERS.
HERE ARE THE ORIGINAL LETTERS FOR WHICH RIVERS WAS BEING BLACKMAILED. ACCORDING TO RIVERS, THEY'RE FORGERIES.
HUMPH!
I HAVE REASON TO BELIEVE THE BLACKMAILER HAD PHOTOSTATS MADE OF THOSE. YOU MIGHT BE ABLE TO LOCATE THE COMMERCIAL PHOTOGRAPHER WHO DID THE JOB.
A SLIM CHANCE, BUT ANYTHING'S WORTH TRYIN'. WE HAVE NO CLUES TO RIVERS'S MURDERER, KIRBY.
ALEX RAYMOND 12-14

OUR HANDWRITING EXPERTS WILL KNOW IF THESE ARE FORGERIES. I HAVE MY DOUBTS. RIVERS WAS A BIT OF A ROUNDER, WASN'T HE?
ROUNDER OR NOT, HE DIED PROTECTING HIS FAMILY-REMEMBER? I'LL BE SEEIN' YOU, SULLY.
Copr. 1946, King Features Syndicate, Inc. World rights reserved.
RIP'S APARTMENT...
THE. PAPERS ARE STILL PLAYING UP THE SWANEE RIVERS MURDER, RIP.
AND PANNING THE POLICE AND ME FOR FAILING TO PUT THE FINGER ON THE KILLER..
Copr. 1946, King Features Syndicate, Inc. World rights reserved.

OH, WELL.. DON'T LET IT THROW YOU. WITH YOU ON THE CASE, THAT KILLER'S DAYS ARE NUMBERED! I KNOW IT!
THANKS, HONEY. YOU'RE GOOD FOR MY MORALE. BUT I WISH WE HAD A CLUE!
IN ANOTHER STATE...
THE RIVERS JOB SURE RAISED A FUSS! WE WERE SMART TO LEAVE TOWN. WHEN ARE YOU GONNA CUT US IN ON THE DOUGH, SPIDER?
WHEN I GET GOOD AN' READY!
ALEX RAYMOND 12-16

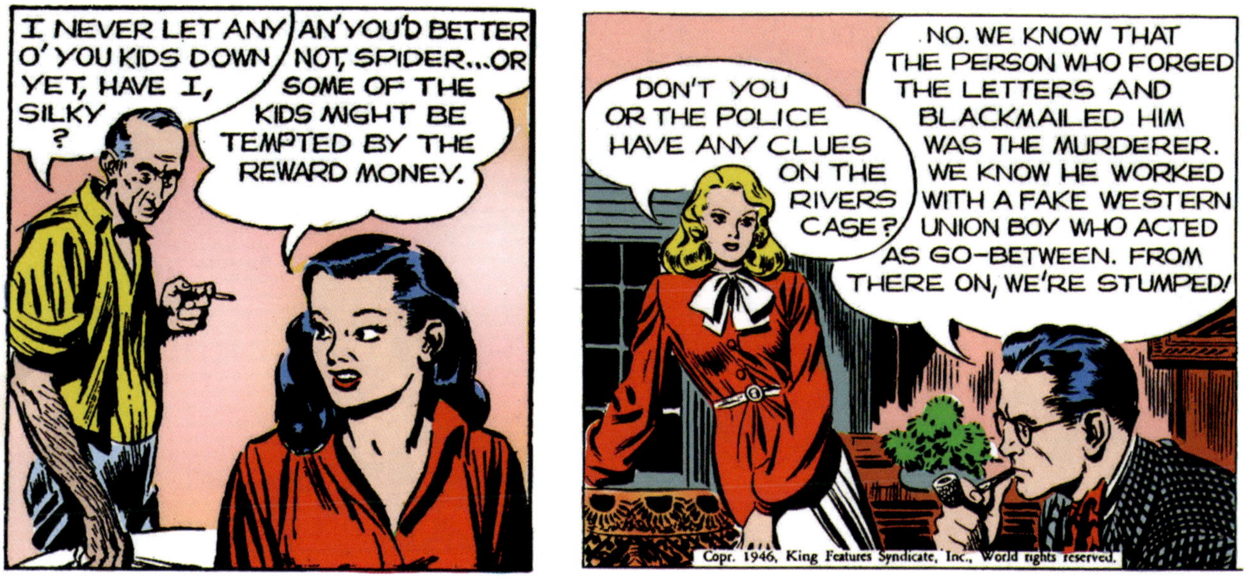
I NEVER LET ANY O' YOU KIDS DOWN YET, HAVE I, SILKY?
AN' YOU'D BETTER NOT, SPIDER...OR SOME OF THE KIDS MIGHT BE TEMPTED BY THE REWARD MONEY.
DON'T YOU OR THE POLICE HAVE ANY CLUES ON THE RIVERS CASE?
NO. WE KNOW THAT THE PERSON WHO FORGED THE LETTERS AND BLACKMAILED HIM WAS THE MURDERER. WE KNOW HE WORKED WITH A FAKE WESTERN UNION BOY WHO ACTED AS GO-BETWEEN. FROM THERE ON, WE'RE STUMPED!
Copr. 1946, King Features Syndicate, Inc., World rights reserved.

BUT NOT LICKED! I'VE NEVER QUIT ON A CASE YET! NOW, IF YOU DON'T MIND, HONEY, WILL YOU RUN ALONG? I HAVE AN IMPORTANT APPOINTMENT..
GOSH! SOUNDS URGENT! NOT A BRUNETTE, I HOPE...
ON HER WAY OUT OF RIP'S APARTMENT BUILDING, HONEY PASSES A GIRL IN THE FOYER...
ALEX RAYMOND 12-17
IT IS A BRUNETTE! IT'S PAGAN LEE! AND SHE SNUBBED ME!

PAROLEE LEE REPORTING, SIR! AND MIGHT I ADD, IT'S A PLEASURE?
DITTO, PAGAN! YOU LOOK LIKE SOMETHING OUT OF A SLICK-PAPER STYLE MAGAZINE!
Copr. 1946, King Features Syndicate, Inc. World rights reserved.
AND EVERYTHING, FROM THE SKIN OUT, BOUGHT WITH HONEST CASH! INCIDENTALLY, I PASSED THE BLONDE CHILD IN THE FOYER ON MY WAY UP...
YOU MEAN HONEY? SHE WOULDN'T LIKE TO KNOW YOU REFERRED TO HER AS A CHILD..DID SHE SEE YOU?
ALEX RAYMOND 12-18

YEAH. BUT I SNUBBED HER..OUT OF MEANNESS! YOU SEE, I'M JEALOUS..I HAVE QUITE A CRUSH ON HER MAN!
HOW HAVE YOU BEEN DOING, PAGAN?
ALL RIGHT. NOT SETTING THE WORLD AFIRE, BUT GIVE ME TIME! I'M SINGING, UNDER AN ASSUMED NAME, IN A JOINT ACROSS THE RIVER..
..A ROMANTIC SPOT, CALLED UTOPIA GARDENS. THEY AVERAGE A BRAWL A NIGHT! WHEN I'M NOT SINGING, I'M PATCHING SPLIT LIPS! BUT THEY LIKE ME.. AND THEY TREAT ME LIKE A LADY!
ALEX RAYMOND 12-19
Copr. 1946, King Features Syndicate, Inc. World rights reserved.
I HOPE TO DO BETTER, RIP...BUT THE MAIN THING IS, I'M MY OWN WOMAN ... AND I'M GOING STRAIGHT.. AND LIKING IT!
AND I'M PROUD OF YOU, PAGAN!
THANK YOU, PAGAN..
RIP, YOUR SAYING YOU'RE PROUD OF ME MEANS A LOT! I WON'T LET YOU DOWN!
Copr. 1946, King Features Syndicate, Inc. World rights reserved.
COME TO THE UTOPIA GARDENS AND WATCH ME WOW THE SUCKERS. I SING UNDER THE NAME OF MADELON. LEAVE THE DORIAN KID AT HOME, THOUGH. IT'S NO PLACE FOR CHILDREN!
HONEY'S A SWEET GIRL, PAGAN. HOW CAN YOU DISLIKE HER SO?

BECAUSE YOU LIKE HER SO MUCH! BECAUSE SHE LOVES YOU! BECAUSE SHE'S EVERYTHING I NEVER WAS OR CAN BE! OH, RIP! YOU'VE HELPED ME SO MUCH! DON'T STOP! I NEED YOU!
I'M HONORED. YOU CAN COUNT ON ME, PAGAN.
ALEX RAYMOND 12-20
WELL! IT'S YOU! DID YOU HAVE AN INTERESTING APPOINTMENT WITH MISS PAGAN LEE?
AREN'T YOU GOING TO INVITE ME IN?
Copr. 1946, King Features Syndicate, Inc. World rights reserved.

IT MAKES PRECIOUS LITTLE DIFFERENCE TO ME WHETHER YOU COME IN OR STAY OUT!
THOUGHT WE'D CATCH THE FLOOR SHOW AT THE UTOPIA GARDENS. THEY HAVE A NEW SINGER. SUPPOSED TO BE GOOD..
I'M SURE MISS LEE WOULD BE DELIGHTED IF YOU ASKED HER
CAN'T. SHE'S THE SINGER!
OF ALL THE NERVE! I WOULDN'T GO IF YOU LET ME THROW ROTTEN TOMATOES AT HER! NOW, PLEASE GO!
OKAY, KIDDO! SORTA HATE TO GO ALONE! GOOD NIGHT!

JEALOUSY OF PAGAN HAS DRIVEN HONEY TO ASK RIP TO LEAVE HER APARTMENT.
OH! HE WENT!
Copr. 1946, King Features Syndicate, Inc. World rights reserved.
GOING DOWN, SIR?
RIP! RIP! WAIT!
PLEASE FORGIVE ME, RIP! I ACTED LIKE A CHILD. IF YOU STILL WANT ME, I'D LOVE TO GO WITH YOU TO HEAR PAGAN SING!
I DO!
YOU DID AND

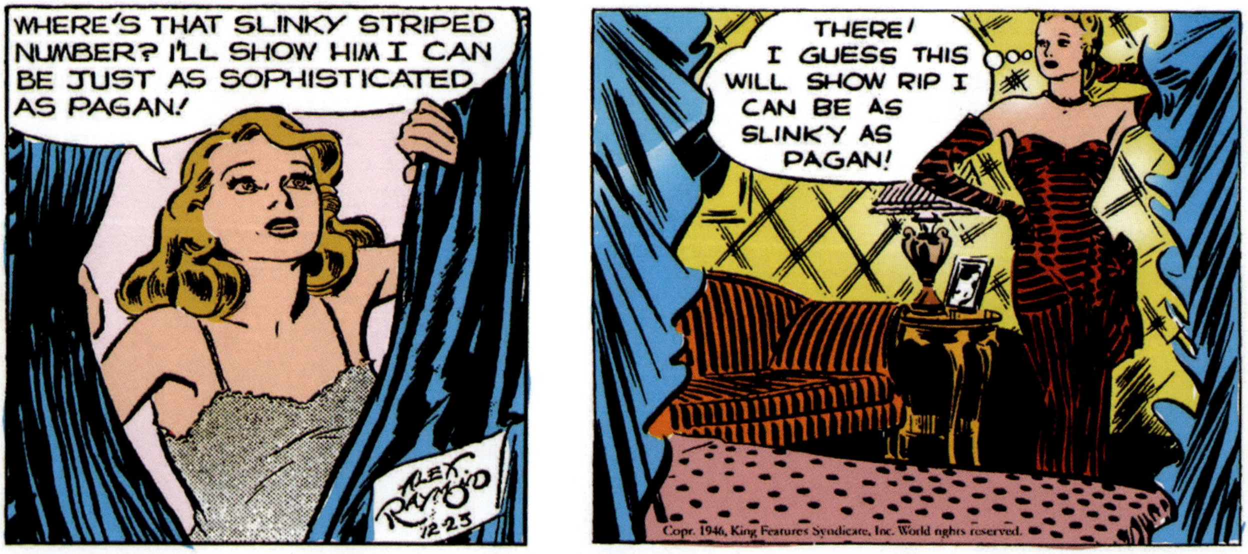
WHERE'S THAT SLINKY STRIPED NUMBER? I'LL SHOW HIM I CAN BE JUST AS SOPHISTICATED AS PAGAN!
ALEX RAYMOND 12-23
THERE! I GUESS THIS WILL SHOW RIP I CAN BE AS SLINKY AS PAGAN!
Copr. 1946, King Features Syndicate, Inc. World rights reserved.

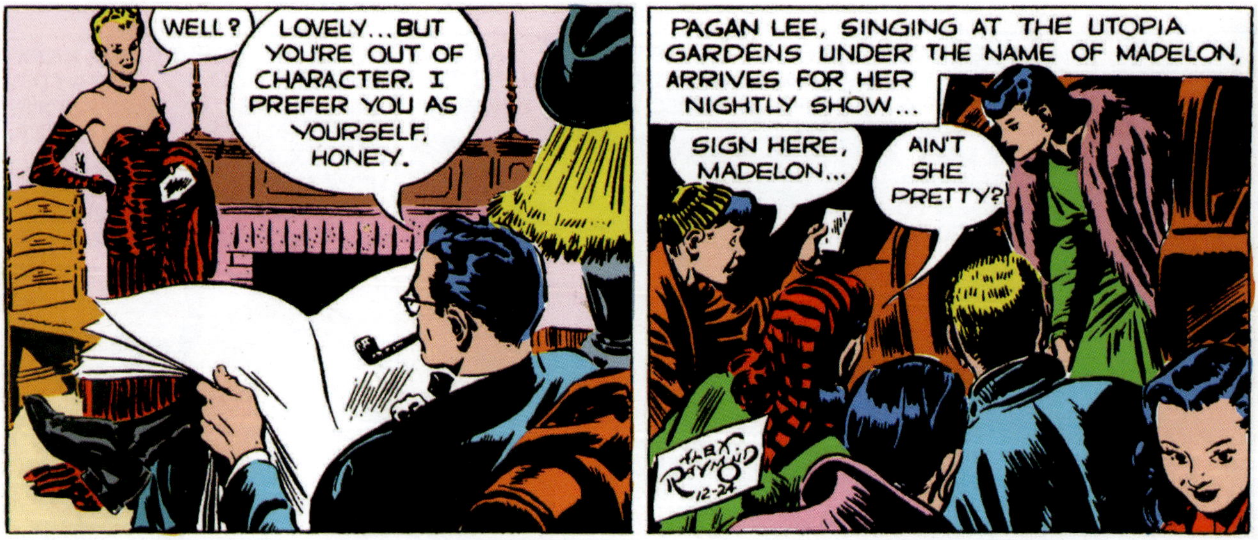
WELL?
LOVELY... BUT YOU'RE OUT OF CHARACTER. I PREFER YOU AS YOURSELF, HONEY.
PAGAN LEE, SINGING AT THE UTOPIA GARDENS UNDER THE NAME OF MADELON, ARRIVES FOR HER NIGHTLY SHOW...
SIGN HERE, MADELON...
AIN'T SHE PRETTY?
ALEX RAYMOND 12-24

HELP! DOORMAN! HELP!
UTOPIA GARDENS
HOODLUMS! MOLEST DECENT CITIZENS, WILL YEZ..?
Copr. 1946, King Features Syndicate, Inc. World rights reserved.

THEY RUINED MY DRESS, THE BRATS!
I'VE SEEN YOU AROUND HERE BEFORE! YOU'RE THE LEADER OF THAT BUNCH! THIS IS MY LAST WARNIN'... KEEP THEM AWAY FROM HERE!
ALEX RAYMOND 12-25
ONE OF A GANG OF AUTOGRAPH KIDS THAT MUSSED UP OUR SINGER MADELON...
MISS SILKY SHAW, EH? UP TO YOUR OLD TRICKS, I SEE!
Copr. 1946, King Features Syndicate, Inc. World rights reserved.

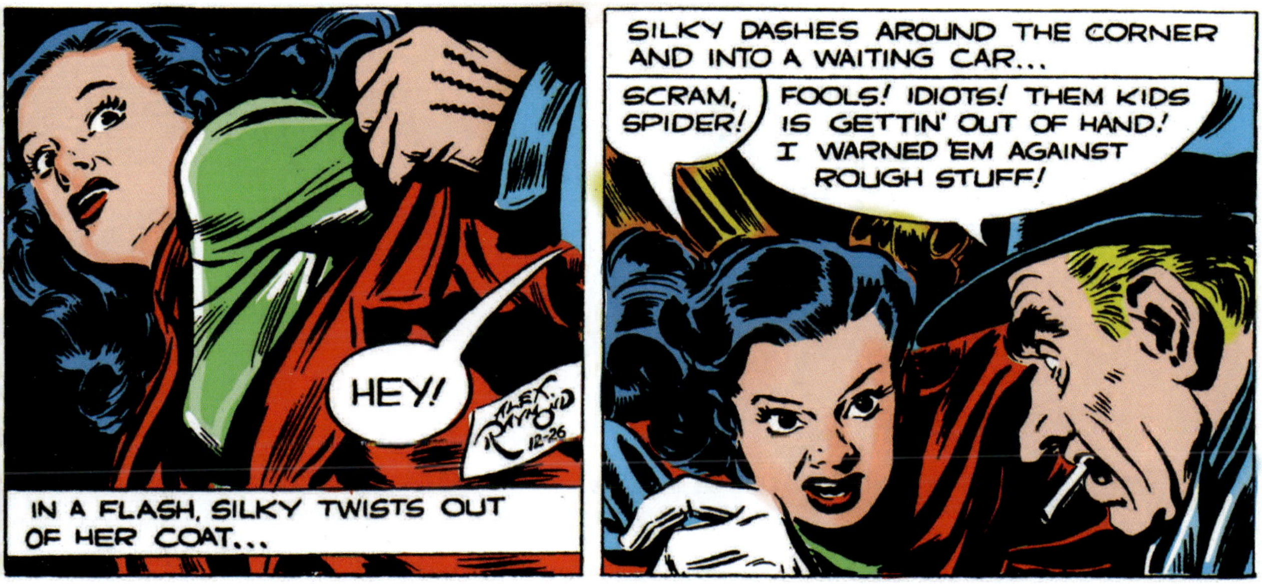
HEY!
ALEX RAYMOND 12-26
IN A FLASH, SILKY TWISTS OUT OF HER COAT...
SILKY DASHES AROUND THE CORNER AND INTO A WAITING CAR...
SCRAM, SPIDER!
FOOLS! IDIOTS! THEM KIDS IS GETTIN' OUT OF HAND! I WARNED 'EM AGAINST ROUGH STUFF!

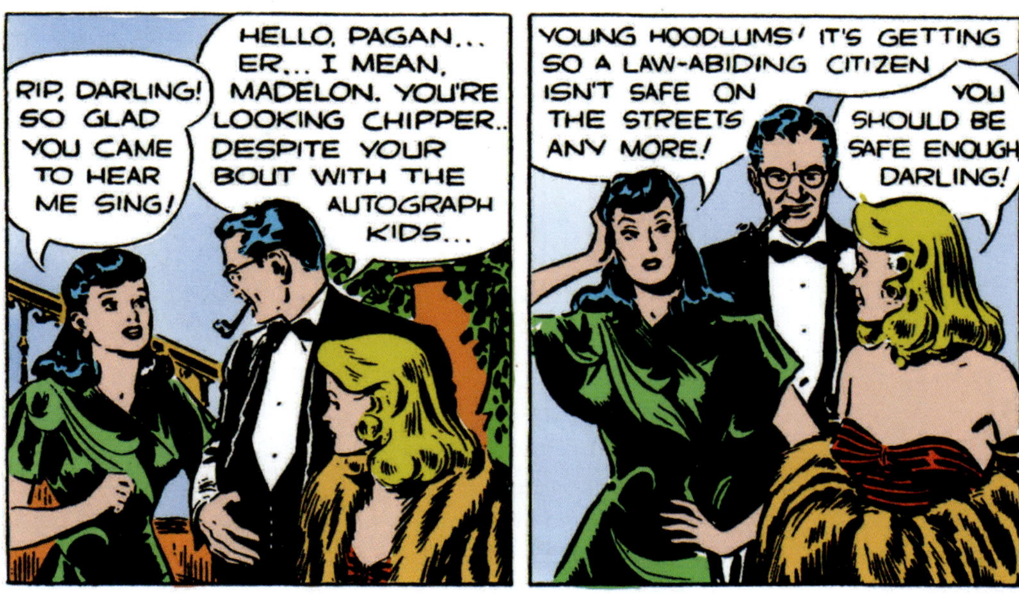
RIP, DARLING! SO GLAD YOU CAME TO HEAR ME SING!
HELLO, PAGAN... ER... I MEAN, MADELON. YOU'RE LOOKING CHIPPER.. DESPITE YOUR BOUT WITH THE AUTOGRAPH KIDS...
YOUNG HOODLUMS! IT'S GETTING SO A LAW-ABIDING CITIZEN ISN'T SAFE ON THE STREETS ANY MORE!
YOU SHOULD BE SAFE ENOUGH, DARLING!

ISN'T IT RATHER LATE FOR THIS CHILD TO BE OUT, RIP?
NOW, NOW, GIRLS, PLEASE!
Copr. 1946, King Features Syndicate, Inc. World rights reserved.
OUTSIDE THE CLUB, SPIDER GRUNT APPROACHES THE DOORMAN...
I'M THE FATHER OF ONE OF THE KIDS WHO MAULED YOUR SINGER THIS EVENING. I WANT TO APOLOGIZE TO HER PERSONALLY.
YOU SHOULD, BUDDY!
ALEX RAYMOND 12-27
THIS GENT SEZ HE'S THE FATHER O' ONE O' THE AUTOGRAPH GOONS THAT MUSSED UP MADELON THIS EVENIN'. WANTS TO SEE HER.
I'LL SEE WHAT I CAN DO MIKE.
Copr. 1946, King Features Syndicate, Inc. World rights reserved.
EXCUSE ME WHILE I SEE THIS MR. SHAW ..I'LL BE RIGHT BACK.
TAKE YOUR TIME, DARLING...THE MORE THE BETTER!
HONEY!
MR SHAW! YOU!
YEAH, PAGAN...OR SHOULD I SAY MADELON? ME, OLD SPIDER GRUNT! YOU AN' ME GOTTA HAVE A TALK, DEARIE!
ALEX RAYMOND 12-28
THIS IS MY DRESSING ROOM. WE CAN TALK IN HERE.
SORRY I HAD TO MASQUERADE UNDER THE NAME OF SHAW, PAGAN, BUT YOU WOULDN'T HAVE SEEN ME, OTHER-WISE...

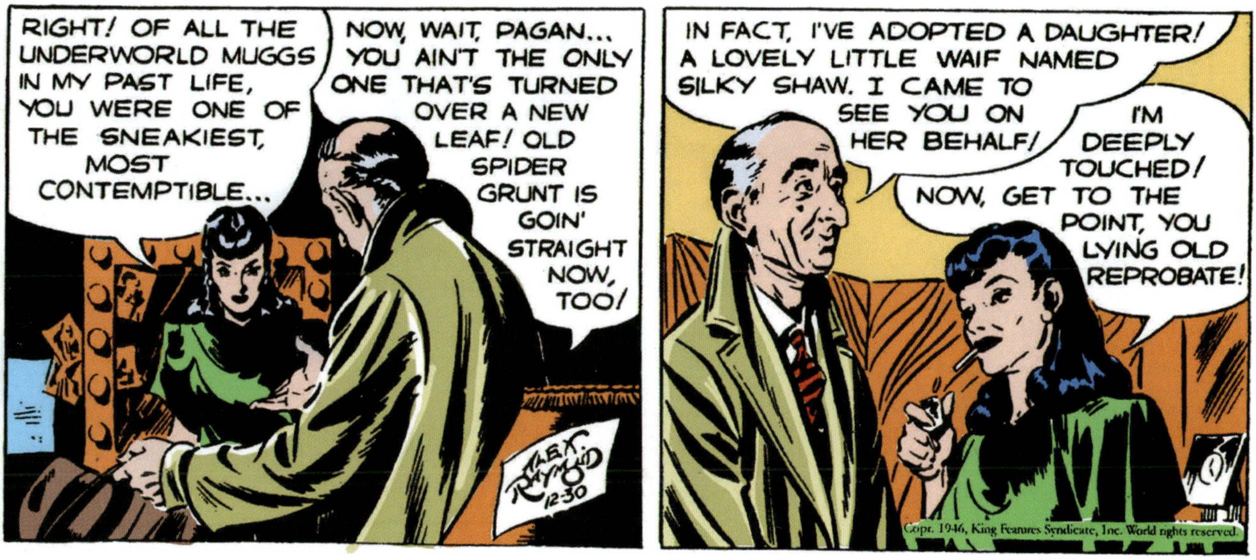
RIGHT! OF ALL THE UNDERWORLD MUGGS IN MY PAST LIFE, YOU WERE ONE OF THE SNEAKIEST, MOST CONTEMPTIBLE...
NOW, WAIT, PAGAN... YOU AIN'T THE ONLY ONE THAT'S TURNED OVER A NEW LEAF! OLD SPIDER GRUNT IS GOIN' STRAIGHT NOW, TOO!
ALEX RAYMOND 12-30
IN FACT, I'VE ADOPTED A DAUGHTER! A LOVELY LITTLE WAIF NAMED SILKY SHAW. I CAME TO SEE YOU ON HER BEHALF!
I'M DEEPLY TOUCHED! NOW, GET TO THE POINT, YOU LYING OLD REPROBATE!
Copr. 1946, King Features Syndicate, Inc. World rights reserved.

SO YOU'RE GOING STRAIGHT! YOU ADOPTED A LITTLE GIRL! WHAT A LINE! COME TO THE POINT, SPIDER... THEN SCRAM, SO I CAN AIR OUT THIS ROOM!
I SEE I'VE MISJUDGED YOU, PAGAN! OF ALL THE PEOPLE I KNEW IN MY SHAMEFUL PAST, I THOUGHT YOU AT LEAST HAD A HEART! VERY WELL... I'LL GO...
WAIT... WHAT DO YOU WANT?
THAT'S MORE LIKE YOU, MY DEAR! MY LITTLE SILKY HAS HEARD YOUR ANGELIC VOICE. SHE IDOLIZES YOU. SHE WAS IN THAT CROWD OF REGRETTABLY ENTHUSIASTIC AUTOGRAPH SEEKERS WHICH MOBBED YOU THIS EVENING...
ALEX RAYMOND 12-31

SHE CAME HOME SOBBING BECAUSE SHE HAD FAILED TO OBTAIN YOUR AUTOGRAPH. I'M HERE TO APOLOGIZE FOR HER AND TO BEG YOU TO MAKE MY LITTLE GIRL HAPPY!
IS THAT ALL YOU WANT? MY AUTOGRAPH?
Copr. 1946, King Features Syndicate, Inc. World rights reserved.
WELL... I CAN'T SEE ANY HARM IN GIVING HER MY AUTOGRAPH...
YES, PAGAN... MY LITTLE SILKY WOULD CHERISH A MEMENTO FROM HER BELOVED MADELON. THAT'S YOUR STAGE NAME, ISN'T IT?

MEANWHILE
PAGAN'S CERTAINLY SPENDING ENOUGH TIME WITH THAT MR. SHAW, HONEY...
HONESTLY, RIP! THE WAY YOU WORRY ABOUT THAT GIRL!
"MR. SHAW!" WONDER IF HE COULD BE ANY RELATION TO OUR LITTLE FRIEND, SILKY SHAW?
OH, PSHAW!
ALEX RAYMOND 1-1
Copr. 1946, King Features Syndicate, Inc. World rights reserved.
AH! THANKS, PAGAN! I KNEW YOU'D DO IT FOR MY LITTLE SILKY. HERE'S MY PEN...
WAIT! I'VE JUST THOUGHT OF SOMETHING! BLACKMAIL IS YOUR RACKET... AND FORGERY...
MY SIGNATURE, PLUS YOUR KNOWLEDGE OF MY PAST, MIGHT MAKE ME A GOOD BLACKMAIL PROSPECT... ESPECIALLY, NOW THAT I'M ON THE WAY UP! I DON'T TRUST YOU, YOU LYING OLD HYPOCRITE! NOW, SCRAM!
NOT WITHOUT YOUR AUTOGRAPH, DEARIE!
MEANWHILE, AT RIP'S TABLE...
MY NAME IS FULWOOD, PREMIER PICTURES. I SAW MADELON SITTING AT YOUR TABLE. COULD YOU INTRODUCE US?
WHY, I'D BE GLAD TO, MR. FULWOOD...
Copr. 1947, King Features Syndicate, Inc. World rights reserved.
YOUR AUTOGRAPH, PAGAN! YOUR STAGE NAME!
WITH A GUN AT MY HEAD, WHAT ELSE CAN I DO?

SOMEONE'S AT THE DOOR.. COME IN!
GET RID OF THEM, BABY! I AIN'T LEAVIN' TILL I GET THAT SIGNATURE!
SORRY TO INTRUDE, PAGAN, BUT MR. FULWOOD HERE, OF PREMIER PICTURES, WANTED TO MEET YOU..
A PLEASURE, GENTLEMEN! THIS IS MR... SHAW...

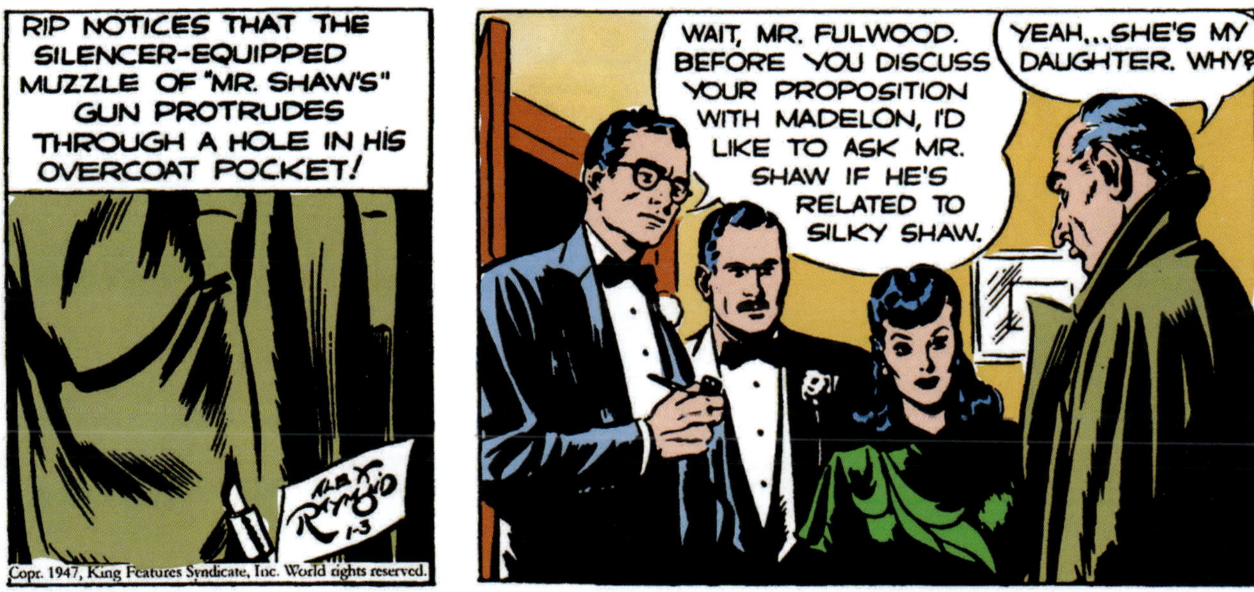
RIP NOTICES THAT THE SILENCER-EQUIPPED MUZZLE OF "MR. SHAW'S" GUN PROTRUDES THROUGH A HOLE IN HIS OVERCOAT POCKET!
Copr. 1947, King Features Syndicate, Inc. World rights reserved.
WAIT, MR. FULWOOD. BEFORE YOU DISCUSS YOUR PROPOSITION WITH MADELON, I'D LIKE TO ASK MR. SHAW IF HE'S RELATED TO SILKY SHAW.
YEAH,..SHE'S MY DAUGHTER. WHY?

I'D ALSO LIKE TO ASK MR. SHAW WHY HE CARRIES A SILENCER-EQUIPPED GUN...THE MUZZLE OF WHICH PROTRUDES THROUGH A HOLE IN HIS POCKET!
AS SPIDER DRAWS HIS GUN, RIP LEAPS... BUT THE HEAVY WEAPON CRASHES AGAINST HIS SKULL!
Copr. 1947, King Features Syndicate, Inc. World rights reserved.

A BLOW ON THE HEAD BY SPIDER GRUNT'S GUN FAILS TO STOP RIP... HIS HURTLING BODY TOPPLES THE FORGER...
Copr. 1947, King Features Syndicate, Inc. World rights reserved.
RIP'S LEFT HAND GRASPS THE CHAMBER OF SPIDER'S REVOLVER, THUS PREVENTING ITS TURNING AND THE GUN'S FIRING...
HIS RIGHT HAND CLAMPS THE WIRY SPIDER'S THROAT....
ALEX RAYMOND 1-6-47
STILL GRASPING SPIDER GRUNT'S GUN AND THROAT, RIP STRUGGLES TO HIS FEET, LIFTING THE FORGER WITH HIM...
THE GUN SLIPS FROM SPIDER'S NERVELESS FINGERS AND RIP FLINGS HIM INTO A CHAIR..

HIS NAME ISN'T SHAW... IT'S SPIDER GRUNT! HE'S A BLACKMAILER AND ONE OF THE CLEVEREST FORGERS IN THE BUSINESS!
SHALL I CALL THE POLICE, KIRBY?
PLEASE, FULWOOD. GET ME LIEUTENANT SULLIVAN AT POLICE HEADQUARTERS.
BEEN TRYIN' TO GET YA, KIRBY. I FOUND THE PHOTOGRAPHER WHO MADE THE PHOTOSTATS IN THE RIVERS CASE...BUT HE SAYS A KID BROUGHT THE STUFF TO HIM...
ALEX RAYMOND 1-8-47

NEVER MIND. COME OUT HERE TO THE UTOPIA GARDENS, SULLY. I THINK I HAVE THE SWANEE RIVERS MURDERER!
YER NUTS, KIRBY! YA CAN'T PIN THE SWANEE RIVERS JOB ON ME!
NO?
YOU'RE A BLACKMAILER AND A FORGER. YOU WORK WITH SILKY SHAW, A VICIOUS LITTLE AUTOGRAPH HOUND. YOU CAME HERE FOR PAGAN'S SIGNATURE. YOU WERE CARRYING A SILENCER-EQUIPPED GUN....
FORGED LOVE LETTERS WERE USED TO BLACKMAIL RIVERS. HE WAS MURDERED WITH A SILENCED GUN! I'M HOLDING YOU ON SUSPICION OF MURDER, SPIDER!
ALEX RAYMOND 1-9-47

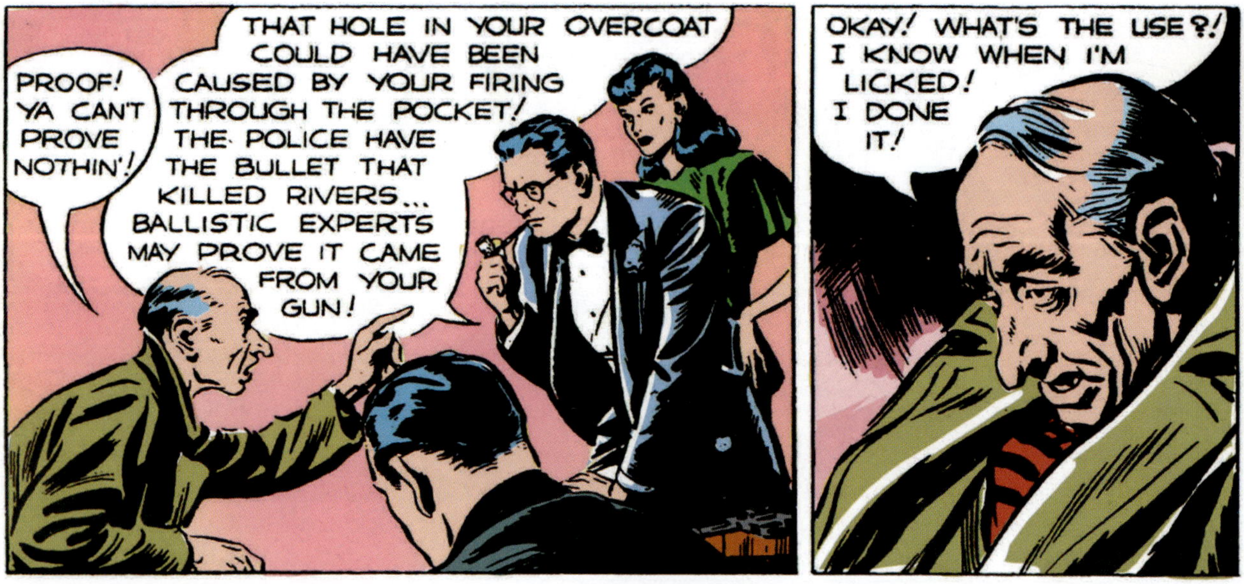
PROOF! YA CAN'T PROVE NOTHIN'!
THAT HOLE IN YOUR OVERCOAT COULD HAVE BEEN CAUSED BY YOUR FIRING THROUGH THE POCKET! THE POLICE HAVE THE BULLET THAT KILLED RIVERS... BALLISTIC EXPERTS MAY PROVE IT CAME FROM YOUR GUN!
OKAY! WHAT'S THE USE?! I KNOW WHEN I'M LICKED! I DONE IT!

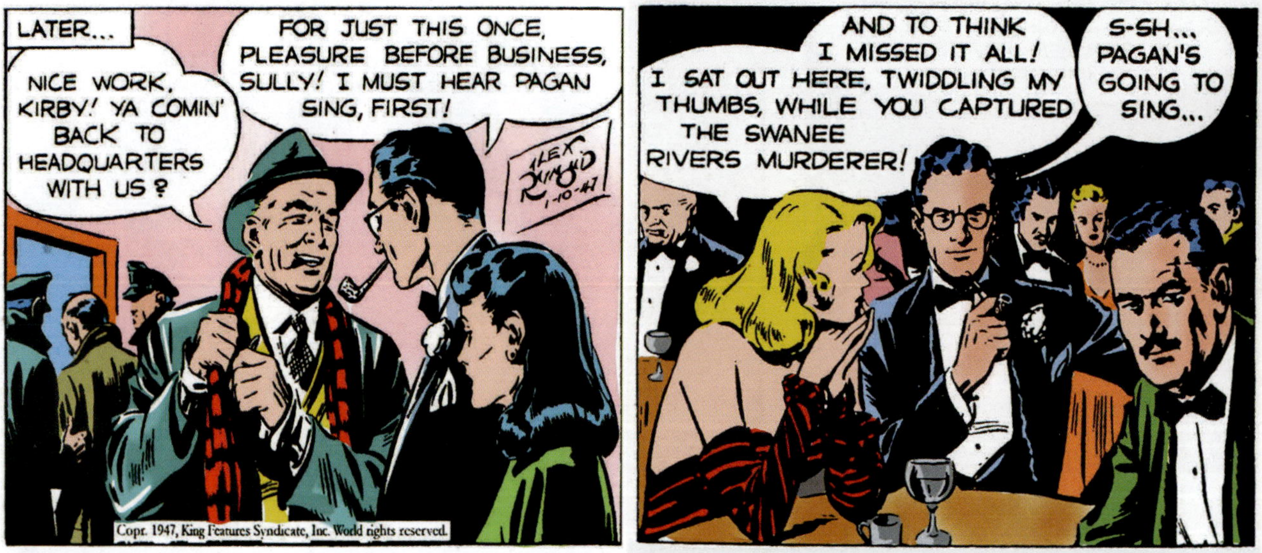
LATER...
NICE WORK, KIRBY! YA COMIN' BACK TO HEADQUARTERS WITH US?
FOR JUST THIS ONCE, PLEASURE BEFORE BUSINESS, SULLY! I MUST HEAR PAGAN SING, FIRST!
AND TO THINK I MISSED IT ALL! I SAT OUT HERE, TWIDDLING MY THUMBS, WHILE YOU CAPTURED THE SWANEE RIVERS MURDERER!
S-SH... PAGAN'S GOING TO SING...

"...AND HE'LL BE TALL AND DARK, THE MAN I LOVE..."
THE HUSSY! SHE'S SINGING TO YOU, RIP!
S-SH!
VOICE, LOOKS, PERSONALITY! SHE HAS WHAT IT TAKES! I'M SIGNING HER WITH PREMIER PICTURES, KIRBY!

NEW YORK CITY...STONE AND STEEL, PULSING WITH THE LIFE OF SEVEN MILLION SOULS ... HUSHED UNDER A SWIRLING CANOPY OF SNOW.
IN ITS STREETS, NEWSBOYS HAWK THE LATEST EXPLOIT OF A PROMINENT CITIZEN...
RIP KOIBY BREAKS SWANEE RIVERS MOIDER CASE! READ ALL ABOUT IT!

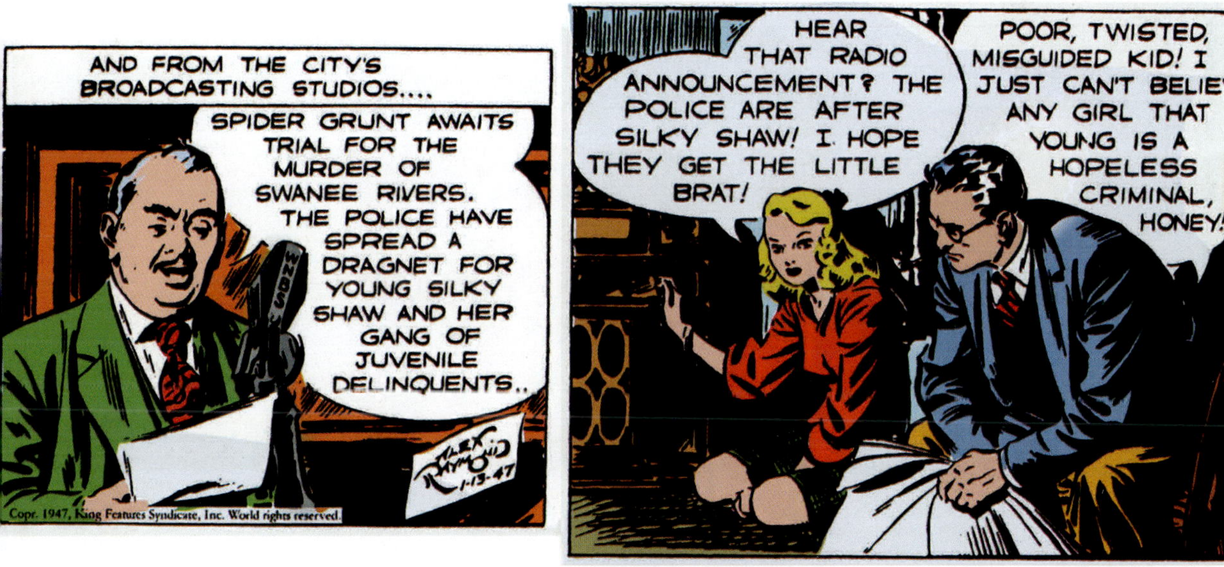
AND FROM THE CITY'S BROADCASTING STUDIOS....
SPIDER GRUNT AWAITS TRIAL FOR THE MURDER OF SWANEE RIVERS. THE POLICE HAVE SPREAD A DRAGNET FOR YOUNG SILKY SHAW AND HER GANG OF JUVENILE DELINQUENTS..
ALEX RAYMOND 1-13-47
Copr. 1947, King Features Syndicate, Inc. World rights reserved.
HEAR THAT RADIO ANNOUNCEMENT? THE POLICE ARE AFTER SILKY SHAW! I HOPE THEY GET THE LITTLE BRAT!
POOR, TWISTED, MISGUIDED KID! I JUST CAN'T BELIEVE ANY GIRL THAT YOUNG IS A HOPELESS CRIMINAL, HONEY!

OUTSIDE, THE DEJECTED FIGURE OF A GIRL TRUDGES THROUGH THE STORM...
ALEX RAYMOND 1-14-47
Copr. 1947, King Features Syndicate, Inc. World rights reserved.
SHE PAUSES MIDWAY ON ONE OF THE CITY'S GREAT BRIDGES AND CONTEMPLATES THE DARK, SWIRLING WATERS FAR BELOW.

THEY GOT SPIDER FOR THE RIVERS MURDER. IT'S JUST A MATTER OF TIME BEFORE THEY NAB ME AS AN ACCOMPLICE...THEN...
Copr. 1947, King Features Syndicate, Inc. World rights reserved.
OH, WHY DIDN'T I LISTEN TO KIRBY'S ADVICE!?NOW IT'S TOO LATE! NO ONE CAN HELP ME!
I'M NO GOOD TO MYSELF OR ANYONE ELSE! THERE'S. ONLY ONE ANSWER...
A GOOD NIGHT TO BE HOME, TOASTIN' ME TOOTSIES AN' SIPPIN' A...
LOOK, CLANCY! SOMEONE'S CLIMBIN' UP ONTO THE RAILIN'!
HOLD ON THERE, SISTER! DON'T BE A FOOL!
Copr. 1947, King Features Syndicate, Inc., World rights reserved.

HELP! GIMME A HAND, CLANCY!
LET GO: I WANT TO DIE!
ALEX RAYMOND 1-16-47
WE PICKED UP THE SHAW KID, JUST AS SHE WAS ABOUT TO JUMP FROM A BRIDGE. SHE WANTS TO SEE YOU, KIRBY.
I'LL BE RIGHT DOWN.
TRIED TO KILL HERSELF? I DON'T BELIEVE IT! NOT THAT VICIOUS LITTLE BRAT! SHE'S JUST TRYING TO GAIN SYMPATHY.
DON'T BE SO HARD ON HER, HONEY!
YOU KNOW I'M NOT HARD, RIP! I JUST DON'T LIKE TO SEE WORTHLESS HUSSIES LIKE SILKY SHAW AND PAGAN LEE WIND MEN AROUND THEIR FINGERS. THE FACT THAT THEY'RE WOMEN SHOULDN'T SWAY YOU..
ALEX RAYMOND 1-17-47
A WOMAN DESERVES NO MORE CONSIDERATION THAN A MAN!
TRUE ENOUGH - BUT ONE MISSTEP SHOULDN'T BAR A WOMAN FROM A SECOND CHANCE!
Copr. 1947, King Features Syndicate, Inc. World rights reserved.
IN A CELL AT POLICE HEADQUARTERS...
OH, MR. KIRBY... I'VE BEEN SO WRONG! ALL I WANT IS ANOTHER CHANCE!
YOU WILL RECALL THAT MISS DORIAN AND I WARNED YOU TO CHANGE YOUR WAYS, AND YOU INSULTED US FOR OUR PAINS...

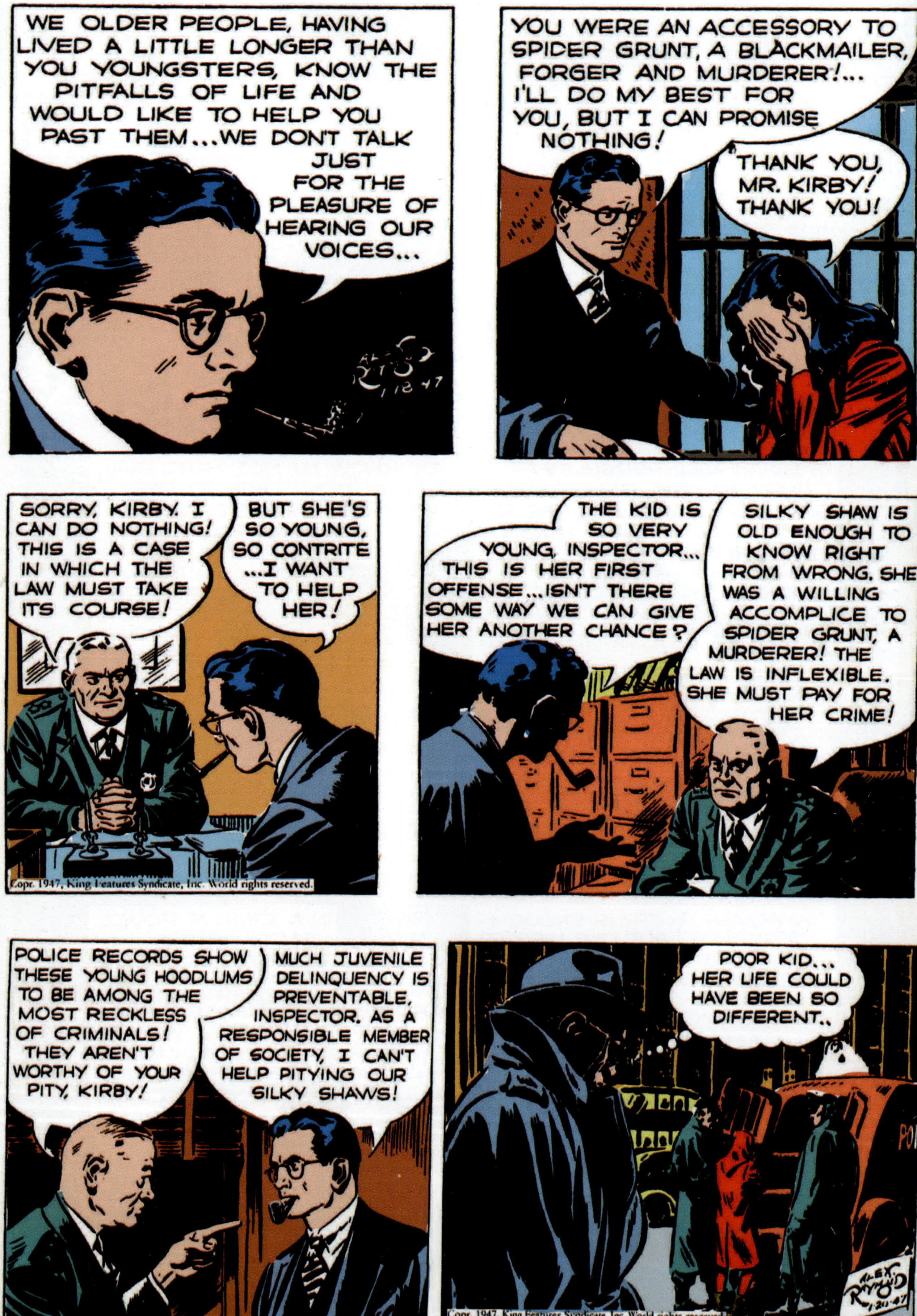
WE OLDER PEOPLE, HAVING LIVED A LITTLE LONGER THAN YOU YOUNGSTERS, KNOW THE PITFALLS OF LIFE AND WOULD LIKE TO HELP YOU PAST THEM...WE DON'T TALK JUST FOR THE PLEASURE OF HEARING OUR VOICES...
YOU WERE AN ACCESSORY TO SPIDER GRUNT, A BLACKMAILER, FORGER AND MURDERER!... I'LL DO MY BEST FOR YOU, BUT I CAN PROMISE NOTHING!
THANK YOU, MR. KIRBY! THANK YOU!
SORRY, KIRBY. I CAN DO NOTHING! THIS IS A CASE IN WHICH THE LAW MUST TAKE ITS COURSE!
BUT SHE'S SO YOUNG, SO CONTRITE ...I WANT TO HELP HER!
Copr. 1947, King Features Syndicate, Inc. World rights reserved.
THE KID IS SO VERY YOUNG, INSPECTOR... THIS IS HER FIRST OFFENSE...ISN'T THERE SOME WAY WE CAN GIVE HER ANOTHER CHANCE?
SILKY SHAW IS OLD ENOUGH TO KNOW RIGHT FROM WRONG. SHE WAS A WILLING ACCOMPLICE TO SPIDER GRUNT, A MURDERER! THE LAW IS INFLEXIBLE. SHE MUST PAY FOR HER CRIME!
POLICE RECORDS SHOW THESE YOUNG HOODLUMS TO BE AMONG THE MOST RECKLESS OF CRIMINALS! THEY AREN'T WORTHY OF YOUR PITY, KIRBY!
MUCH JUVENILE DELINQUENCY IS PREVENTABLE, INSPECTOR. AS A RESPONSIBLE MEMBER OF SOCIETY, I CAN'T HELP PITYING OUR SILKY SHAWS!
POOR KID... HER LIFE COULD HAVE BEEN SO DIFFERENT..
ALEX RAYMOND 1-20-47
Copr. 1947, King Features Syndicate, Inc. World rights reserved.